The College Student's Research Companion

by
Arlene Rodda Quaratiello

Neal-Schuman Publishers, Inc.
New York   London

Published by Neal-Schuman Publishers, Inc.
100 Varick Street
New York, NY 10013

Printed and bound in the United States of America

Library of Congress Cataloging-in-Publication Data

Quartatiello, Arlene Rodda.
   The college student's research companion / by Arlene Rodda Quaratiello.
      p. cm.
   Includes bibliographical references and index.
   ISBN 1–55570–275–9
   1. Libraries—United States. 2. Searching, Bibliographical.
3. Report writing. I. Title.
Z710.Q37   1997
025.5'24—DC21
                                          97–18811
                                            CIP

Dedication

This book is dedicated to my husband Mark, whose emotional support and technical assistance smoothed out the long road I traveled while writing it.

Contents

Permissions

Material from the *Readers' Guide to Periodical Literature* and *Biography Index* © H.W. Wilson Co. Reprinted with the permission of the H.W. Wilson Company.

FirstSearch Web pages © OCLC. Reprinted with the permission of OCLC. FirstSearch is a trademark of the Online Computer Library Center, Inc. *Newspaper Abstracts* is a product of UMI, a Bell & Howell company.

Expanded Academic ASAP ™ screens © 1996 Information Access Co. Full text of the *Washington Monthly* © *Washington Monthly*. Reprinted with the permission of the Washington Monthly Co., 1611 Connecticut Ave. NW, Washington, D.C. 20009, (202) 462-0128.

Readers' Guide Abstracts screens © H.W. Wilson Co. Reprinted with the permission of the H.W. Wilson Company.

PsycLIT screens:

© 1986-1995 American Psychological Association. Reprinted with the permission of the American Psychological Association, publisher of *Psychological Abstracts* and the *PsycINFO* database (copyright 1967-1996). All rights reserved.

© 1986-1995 SilverPlatter International N.V. Reprinted with the permission of SilverPlatter.

Netscape screens © Netscape Communications Corp. Reprinted with the permission of Netscape Communications Corp. Netscape Communications, the Netscape Communications logo, *Netscape*, and *Netscape Navigator* are trademarks of Netscape Communications Corp.

Figures and Tables

FIGURES

TABLES

Preface

I wrote *The College Student's Research Companion* because of the frustration I encountered when I tried to teach students the basics of library research in a single class period. Because of the increasing complexity of libraries, I barely had time to touch upon the essential principles they needed to know before my time was up. I began to wish that the students attending my instructional sessions, most of whom knew very little about libraries and research, could have come with a bit more background so that we could make the most of the time available.

With these feelings, I began to write a book that could explain to students the fundamental logic common to using any academic library. I tried as much as possible to avoid focusing on details that would quickly become outdated and irrelevant, instead concentrating on the underlying concepts that would not change. With a thorough understanding of these concepts, readers will become more confident in dealing with the rapid pace of technological change as they realize that much about research actually stays the same.

My philosophy throughout *The College Student's Research Companion* is that information should be judged for what it conveys, not how it is conveyed. In other words, an older article on microfilm may be more valuable for a certain project than a recent article found through an online service; an encyclopedia volume may answer a question more quickly and thoroughly than a search of the Web; a print index may provide better citations for a particular subject than an electronic one. Selecting sources regardless of their format results in higher quality research and better research papers.

This book guides the reader through the research process from topic selection in the first chapter to the evaluation and citing of resources in the final chapter. The first five chapters of the book focus primarily on book resources and includes a discussion of how to use online catalogs, and how to physically locate the books, as well as an overview of some major reference sources. Following this information are several chapters which concentrate primarily on finding articles. A discussion of periodical indexes in their various formats as well as some tips on obtaining the articles are included in this section. Chapter 8 will help you to learn to use the Internet as a research tool and explain the basics of searching the World Wide Web and the types of information found on the Web. It is critical today to be familiar with *all* the ways in which you can locate information.

Throughout *The College Student's Research Companion* I draw many comparisons between doing library research and going on a "road trip." I believe that research is a journey of discovery which can be just as exciting and stimulating as a road trip to an unknown destination. Too many students are intimidated or bored by library research. These are the ways that most people react to things they don't understand. My hope is that this book will contribute to the readers' understanding of libraries, help them to attain the skills necessary to find information that leads to knowledge, and instill in them an appreciation of library research that will enable them to "enjoy the ride."

Introduction

Back in 1984—so long ago that there were still *card* catalogs in libraries—I went away to college, eager to expand both my intellectual outlook and, perhaps more important to me at the time, my social horizons. As I look back upon that first difficult yet exciting week of freshman year, I see a blur of images involving going to parties at night where nobody really knew anyone else, and then going to classes during the day, feeling as if there would be no way I could do all of my work. After drinking too much, sleeping too little, eating tasteless dining-hall food, and spending my life savings on textbooks, I walked into the library for the first time and thought that I had never seen so many books.

Over the next four years, I spent a good deal of time in that venerable building, mostly as a work-study student shelving books, sending out overdue notices, and performing other hazardous duties. I actually did most of my studying in the dorms, either in my own room or that of a friend. During my senior year, I found the college pub to be a great study lounge in the early evening before it took on its primary function. But occasionally I had to do some research in the library. Although I had always loved to browse in libraries, I didn't know very much about research in those days, and, as a result, I experienced a great deal of frustration and wasted a lot of time. I would much rather have spent that time enjoying what my friends and I often referred to facetiously as "extended study breaks."

Aside from hanging out at great length in each other's rooms drinking coffee or cheap wine, these extended study breaks often took the form of road trips—a jaunt through central Massachusetts on an Indian Summer Sunday afternoon, a drive to Cape Cod on an unseasonably warm spring day—you get the picture. Toward the end of the semester, with exams looming, we sometimes even brought our textbooks along on our little excursions and justified our actions by convincing ourselves that we would study outside. But, of course, the books remained unopened, and we returned to campus with a mild sense of guilt, admitting reluctantly that we would have gotten more studying done if we had gone to the library. Still, my fondest memories of college are certainly not of the library but of those spontaneous excursions my friends and I used to take.

When I started writing *The College Student's Research Companion*, I was inspired by these memories and began to appreciate certain similarities between taking a road trip and the whole process of doing a research paper. Superficially, the two would seem to have nothing in common. But consider this. My friends and I usually had some idea of where we were going—a beach, a park, an all-night pancake house—even though our excursions often just seemed like joyrides. In a basic sense, we planned the route we would take to get to our destination, whether it was along the back roads or on the highway. Finally, we needed some form of transportation. During any given semester, fortunately, one of us had a functioning vehicle.

In the same way, you must choose a destination when you begin your research; this is your topic. You then plan your route by determining how you will proceed through the library to find what you need. And, most essentially, you must know how to use the library's resources just as you would need to know how to drive a car if you were to go on a road trip. This *Companion* will teach you how to do all of these things.

Although I said that my most memorable experiences occurred well beyond the walls of the library, I do have one very vivid library memory, though it's hardly a fond one. During my senior year, I had to take an environmental science course for nonmajors in order to fulfill a core requirement. The professor assigned a research paper. As an English major, I had never researched any scientific topics, so I was particularly intimidated by the prospect of having to go over to the recently constructed, ultramodern science library. In order to make maximum use of the space in this new library, compact shelving had been installed—the type of shelving that closes up so there are no aisles in between the book stacks. If you need a book on a particular shelf, you crank open the appropriate shelving unit and walk in. Well, I guess I didn't do this properly, because after I walked in to get the book, the shelves started closing in on me. I thought my college career and my life would end at that moment, and the potential headline of the student newspaper flashed before my eyes: "Crushed in the Stacks!" Fortunately, I was able to muster enough strength to push the shelves apart for a moment, long enough to escape.

You would think that after such a traumatic experience, I would have developed a fear of libraries. But I didn't. In fact, I went on to graduate school and got a master's degree in library science. Why would I do such a thing? Well, during my four years as an undergraduate, I realized how little I knew and how little I would ever be able to know. The amount of information you can store in your head is trivial compared to the amount of information that actually exists. These discouraging thoughts began to arise the minute I first stepped into the college library. But fortunately, we do have libraries to store all of this information. I realized, perhaps a bit late, that knowing how to tap the resources contained in these warehouses of knowledge is a powerful skill to possess in our information society.

I now work as a reference librarian and teach students how to find the information they need with ease and efficiency, saving them a lot of time and frustration. I have seen countless students come into the library with apprehensive expressions on their faces. I used to wonder what horrible library experiences they had endured, speculating that maybe they too had had frightening encounters with compact shelving. But soon I realized that it was probably just the idea of having to do a research paper that was overwhelming them. Today, more than ever, as information explodes all around us, and a bewildering variety of new computerized resources emerges to handle it all, the library can indeed be an intimidating place.

The College Student's Research Companion is intended to be your travel guide in a figurative sense, a guide to make the library a less intimidating place by showing you the way to go. In the chapters that follow, I'll pass along some tips so that you won't get lost in the unfamiliar surroundings of college libraries. With the techniques you'll learn by reading this book, I hope that doing research will become a positive and, dare I say, even an enjoyable experience for you.

One

Hitting the Road

CHOOSING YOUR DESTINATION

Picture the following student. She assertively comes up to the Reference Desk and says, "I'm writing a research paper about the prevalence of supernatural television shows during the '60s; you know, like *Gilligan's Island, I Dream of Jeannie, The Addams Family.* I need to give some background on the shows themselves and then explain why this became such a popular genre during that particular decade. So how can I find some information on this?"

Now imagine another student. He hesitantly approaches the Reference Desk after wandering around the library for a while and asks, "So where's the TV section? I've got a huge paper due tomorrow and I gotta find some stuff quick!"

Who do you suppose will have more success in researching this paper?

I have observed that students who seem confused and overwhelmed don't really know what they're looking for in the first place. Many students walk into the library with a paper assignment and no idea of what to do next. Maybe they don't even understand the assignment or are feeling apathetic about it. These are the people who are most likely to be frustrated and develop a negative attitude about the library. At the opposite end of the spectrum are those students who have a clear idea of their topic and what approach they

1

want to take in addressing it, and they are not afraid to ask for help. Their enthusiasm will enable them to surmount the inevitable roadblocks along the way.

The most crucial step in the research process is defining what it is you're looking for, just as you first choose a destination when planning a trip. This is necessary to give you a firm foundation. Both students mentioned earlier have been given similar assignments: to write a research paper about some topic relating to television. The first student has selected a narrow topic about which to write, probably something that holds some personal interest for her. She has a clear idea of where she's headed. The second student hasn't nailed down a topic yet, and so he has no idea what information he really needs. He thinks that if he goes to the library and browses through the section of books about television, he'll find what he needs. But he's probably going to have a difficult time.

When selecting a topic, it's always wise to choose something that will engage your curiosity, something that will motivate you when the going gets rough. When you plan a trip, for example, you naturally are drawn toward a place that appeals to you. In the same way, pick a paper topic that appeals to you. Think about the discussions in your classes that were interesting, or something that you read in your textbook that you would like to pursue further, or just something of personal interest.

Even if you're not given a great deal of latitude in choosing a topic for a particular class assignment, you can come up with a "twist" that will make researching the assigned topic interesting. For instance, let's say you have to do a paper about some aspect of ancient Greek civilization. Unless you're a history or classics major, this assignment probably doesn't sound too thrilling. But perhaps you are interested in sports. How about doing some research on the ancient Olympic Games and the role that sport played in Greek society?

Once you feel that you have zoomed in on an interesting

subject, write down a brief *statement* of this topic. For example: "Supernatural television shows of the '60s and why they became so popular during that time." These topic statements might eventually even serve as your paper's title. Then write down the major questions that you'll want to answer. To continue with the preceding example, here are a few questions that the student will probably need to address:

- What were the titles of these supernatural shows, and what was each one about?
- How long was each on the air, and how popular were they?
- What was going on in the sixties (in society, culture, politics, and so on) that might explain the popularity of this genre?

If you can write questions down in a coherent manner, you'll have a clear understanding of your needs. The process of writing will also make your destination more concrete.

You don't have to pinpoint your topic to the minutest detail. In fact, if you're too narrow in your selection, you will limit yourself. Finding that balance between too broad and too narrow is an art that is often mastered through trial and error. You may find that once you start your research, your original topic will evolve into something different from what you had imagined. Something you come across in your reading may take you down another road. But such detours don't have to take you out of your way—in fact, they often take you on a short cut to your ultimate goal.

Just remember, if you don't know where you're going, you'll probably never get there. This holds true on the road as well as in the library.

PLANNING YOUR ROUTE

After you've determined your topic, you are ready to map out your route. In other words, you should identify the types of sources that will provide you with the information you need, determine where you will find these sources, and estimate how much time you will need to do your research.

Why should you have a plan? Well, without one, you'll probably just end up browsing through the library. Although browsing can be effective in the very preliminary phase of research by helping you to select a topic and perhaps find some general information, it's not a very good method to use once you've chosen a topic, especially if your topic is very narrow. So think of browsing as a joyride: you have no particular destination but you may see some interesting things along the way. I have nothing against browsing; in fact, I love it. But I have observed some students who come in the day before a paper is due and try to get information by flipping through issues of magazines or by wandering through a section of the library that seems to have books relating to their subjects. This usually doesn't work very well.

Books

For most topics, of course, finding books will be an essential component of your research. There are two types of books in the library: those you can take out and those you can't—also known as circulating books and reference books, respectively. In the first part of this book, I'll explain how to use an online catalog most efficiently to find books on your topic. Then, I'll take you on a tour through the stacks— those rooms filled with shelves and shelves of books—and explain how everything is organized. Finally, I'll point out the most useful reference books for college students' research papers. Encyclopedias, handbooks, yearbooks, and the like can be great sources for quick and concise factual information, and many are now becoming available in computerized formats.

Periodicals

Finding articles in periodicals (such as newspapers, magazines, scholarly journals) is another essential component of doing research. In fact, sometimes periodicals provide the only information on very narrow or very current topics. For example, let's suppose that you're doing a paper examining the ways in which small businesses are utilizing the Internet. What types of sources would you use to find information? Because of the currency of the topic, I don't think you would find too many useful books. Instead, you would want to rely more heavily on periodicals. To find articles in periodicals, you would need to select appropriate indexes (as I'll explain in chapter 5). Depending on the computer resources of your library, you would have to make choices about which CD-ROM or online databases to use (I'll explain how to make these choices in chapter 6). My point at the moment is simply for you to realize that you will have many decisions to make as you plan your route.

The Internet

The Internet, that worldwide network of computers that has made its way to just about every college campus, is becoming an increasingly common research tool. Although it's not yet the global electronic library that it's often hyped to be, there is a great deal of interesting material available on the Internet, and its resources are expanding at an exponential rate. The World Wide Web, an easy-to-use graphical system for obtaining Internet information, is rapidly increasing in popularity. For such a topic as the Internet and small business, the Web would be an excellent place to look for information.

Other Libraries

Planning your route will also involve decisions such as whether to go to another library. Since not every library can buy every book or subscribe to every periodical, you may have to go elsewhere for the books you need, particularly if another college library has a special collection that relates to your subject. Many smaller academic libraries select books based upon the academic programs of the school. So a college that specializes in technology will have a lot of science books, but maybe not so many books on literature and fine arts. Fortunately, most libraries are members of a consortium—a group of libraries in the same area that share resources. You can also get materials that you need through Interlibrary Loan (ILL), a service that locates a hard-to-find book or article elsewhere in the country and delivers it to your library. This is a helpful service, but you usually have to allow a week or two for the material to arrive. If you're strapped for time, you can also order articles for a fee through such computerized services as UnCover and FirstSearch, both of which will be explained later.

Planning Your Time

Another important aspect of the planning stage is determining how long you will need to do your research and complete your paper. Although waiting until the last minute is a college tradition, expect to be particularly stressed if you do this. The research process is a time-consuming one, no matter how many time-saving hints I give you.

Although computers are a tremendous aid, they don't just spit out the exact information you need without some mental effort on your part. And you can't yet get all the information you need on a computer screen. Although an increasing number of computer databases provide the text of articles right on the screen and electronic versions of entire books are available on the Internet, you will very likely actually have to get your hands on a lot of the material you need. This requires time and effort.

The length of the paper as well as your own research experience will, of course, determine when you should start your research. I have no mathematical formula to offer you concerning how many days you'll need to complete a certain number of pages. My primary recommendation is that you allow yourself time for roadblocks along the way: a book you need has been checked out; you realize that you'll have to go to another library; you need to get a book through Interlibrary Loan; there are any number of scenarios. Sometimes your gut instincts will tell you when it's time to start. When I was in college, I knew it was time to do a paper when a mild anxiety came over me. Since I have always found that the cure for worry is action, just getting started on a paper would make me feel better. I always managed to get my papers done with time to spare so I could get a decent night's sleep instead of pulling an all-nighter.

YOUR MEANS OF TRANSPORTATION

Once you have pinpointed your information needs and made a plan for finding that information, you'll also need the means to find it—just as you'd need a car to get to your destination. To do effective research, you have to know how to use the traditional library, but you should also familiarize yourself with the new technologies I have already mentioned. In addition to knowing the basics of how libraries are organized, you will find it very helpful to know how to operate such things as computerized catalogs, CD-ROMs, and online databases. Considering the potential of the information superhighway to transform the library as we know it today, it is also important to understand the trends in this direction, and to be familiar with the Internet and World Wide Web.

Learning how to use all of these resources is not something you want to do right before a paper is due. You didn't learn how to drive a car for one particular trip, did you? You need to become familiar with the library even before your first assignment is assigned. Even if you don't have a particular assignment yet, stop by the library and get acquainted. Try out all of the electronic resources. Practice using your library's computers by looking up a subject of personal interest. Go on a tour if they're being offered. If you are given the opportunity to go to an instructional session at the library, consider yourself fortunate, because these classes can be enormously helpful. And, finally, of course, read the rest of this book. The time you invest now in learning how to navigate through the library will save you a great deal of frustration in the future.

A FEW WORDS ABOUT THE EXAMPLES USED IN THIS BOOK

The car in which you learned to drive may not be the car you drive now. But because all cars operate according to the same basic principles, you'll find that things are fundamentally the same: you put your foot on the gas pedal to make the car accelerate, or on the brake to slow down or stop; you turn the wheel to steer. Sure, little things are different: on a dark night when it starts to rain and you're driving someone else's car, you may curse as you search frantically for the windshield wiper controls. And you'll probably need a few extra lessons to learn how to drive a standard if you're accustomed to an automatic. In the future perhaps, as you sit behind the wheel of your flashy new electronic automobile, you may look upon that driver's ed car as an antique, but the lessons you learned in that gas-powered vehicle should still be easily transferable.

The examples used in this book can be like that driver's ed car. Although you may not use exactly the same resources in your library, the examples I have chosen demonstrate fundamental principles that will enable you to use the particular resources that are at your disposal. It is unavoidable that the sources I cover in the rapidly changing world of information technology will undergo minor as well as drastic modifications by the time you read this book. But I believe that most of these changes will be superficial, just as the look of cars has been altered over the years but the way you drive them hasn't changed very much. That's why it's so important to understand the basic theories of doing research rather than the specifics. Another important thing to note is that the number of items retrieved in particular examples is the amount I got when doing the search. These numbers would obviously be different if the same search were done now, since resources are constantly updated.

Think of it like this. You may have had the experience of sitting down at a computer terminal in your library one day and returning the next to find that what you see on the screen and the way in which you interact with the computer has changed. Major changes are occurring right now as many electronic resources are becoming accessible over the World Wide Web. Computers are constantly being upgraded and supposedly improved, but this leaves the average user feeling confused and intimidated. My purpose, therefore, in using certain examples will be to demonstrate the fundamentals that endure, rather than giving you specific instructions that might change by next week. With the knowledge of the underlying theories, you will have a road map that will lead you through unfamiliar territory.

Two

A Set of Keys for the Online Catalog

A s you have probably noticed, the card catalog has become a relic in most libraries. There are still a few around, but for the most part they have become about as outdated as a Model-T Ford. They have been replaced by *online catalogs*, which are sometimes also referred to as *OPACs* (online public access catalogs).

Library users relate to these online catalogs in surprisingly different ways. Some welcome this technology as they would a brand new car, realizing that computers provide a more efficient means of retrieving information. But others, who figuratively prefer walking to their destination despite the inconvenience and waste of time, hesitate to touch any of the keys out of fear that the computer terminal will bite them. Between these two extremes, of course, are many variations. Depending on where you fall within this spectrum, I hope that this chapter will either increase your appreciation and understanding of computerized library catalogs or at least lessen your apprehension of them. The points I'll cover here will provide you with the keys you'll need to operate whatever system is in use at your library. In fact, with these keys you will more fully understand all the other computerized resources described in this book.

ONLINE CATALOG BASICS

The Structure of Online Catalogs

Each item in a particular library has a *record* in the online catalog. Items are usually books, although there may of course be other types of material catalogued by the library, such as videos and CDs. All of these records together comprise the *database* of the library's holdings.

Just as a database is composed of individual records, each record is composed of individual elements called *fields*. A field is a certain type of information about the item, be it a book or some other kind of material. There is usually a title field, a subject field, a publisher field, and so on. Another very important field is the call number, which, as I'll detail in chapter 3, indicates the location of the book in the library. Figure 2.1 displays an example of a book record; note the different fields.

```
MATERIAL:       Book

CALL NUMBER:    PS3521.E735.O5 1991

AUTHOR:         Kerouac, Jack, 1922-1969.

TITLE:          On the road/Jack Kerouac; introduction by Ann
                Charters.

PUBLICATION:    New York, N.Y., U.S.A.: Penguin Books, 1991.

DESCRIPTION:    xxxiii, 310 p.; 20 cm.

SERIES:         Penguin twentieth-century classics

NOTES:          Includes bibliographical references (p. [xxxi]-
                xxxiii).

SUBJECT:        Beat generation--Fiction
```

Figure 2.1: An online catalog record for a copy of *On the Road*

Although technically an online catalog is the database itself, not the individual computer you use to search the database, in some libraries the computer or terminal may also be called the online catalog. *Online,* by the way, is a computer term that simply refers to the connection between computers: when a computer is online it can retrieve information from any other computer to which it is properly connected. All the online catalog terminals in a particular library are hooked up to a main computer known as a *server.* This server stores the database containing the records for all the items in that library. It has become increasingly common for students with their own computers to be able to connect to the server and search the online catalog from their homes, dorms, and other remote locations.

It also may be possible for you to search the online catalogs of other libraries without leaving your own library if the online terminals provide access to outside catalogs as well as your own. Or, if your library is a member of a consortium, there may be one single online catalog database that includes the records for all the items in all the member libraries. Increasingly you will notice that libraries offer more than just online catalogs on their online terminals. For instance, you may also be able to access periodical indexes, hop on the Internet, or use other online resources I will cover in upcoming chapters. Although I will be focusing in this chapter on techniques used primarily for searching online catalogs, many of these principles apply to searching all electronic databases.

Dealing with the Online Catalog

Always remember that the online catalog is simply a tool. Like all computerized resources, it is really very stupid and can do nothing unless it is instructed to do something by the user. These instructions are given by entering commands. The computer will respond by displaying information on the terminal screen.

Have patience as you familiarize yourself with a new online catalog. Most of them are designed for the *end user* (that means you), so you certainly shouldn't need to have a degree in computer science to figure them out. Although I think some people get a little overwhelmed when the screen appears to be complicated, this complexity is to insure that everything you need to know to proceed to the next step is displayed right there on the screen. If you read these onscreen instructions instead of glossing over them, you will be better off. There is also usually a "help" command of some sort, if you need further directions. And don't forget that librarians are around to help you too.

If you've never used a computer before in any context or are not very experienced, don't be intimidated. If I didn't know how to drive a car, I'd probably be hesitant to get behind the wheel and take it for a spin, but that's because I might crash into a tree and bash my skull. I assure you that nothing so terrible will happen if you press the wrong key on the computer keyboard.

SEARCHING TECHNIQUES

Although the layout and format of online catalogs in different libraries may vary, fundamentally they all operate in the same way. As in the old card catalog days, there are three basic ways of finding a book: by title, by author, and by subject. Computers, however, have made possible a whole new way of searching called keyword searching, which makes it easier to find material that might elude you through traditional searching techniques.

By Title or Author

It is easiest to find a book if you know the author's name or the exact title. There are a couple of simple conventions to use when searching for books by author or title. When looking up an author, use the last name first, as in **King Stephen** (usually no comma is necessary). When looking up a title, the general rule is to drop any articles (**A Tale of Two Cities** becomes **Tale of Two Cities**). If the computer doesn't find what you're looking for, check to see if you have the correct spelling and word order. As I said before, the computer is dumb. If you misspell the author Mark Twain as Mark Twin, the computer will not assume you are looking for Twain (as a person might easily deduce). The computer takes the commands you give it quite literally. If there's a typo or a word out of place, it can't help you. Other than this, searching by author or title is really quite straightforward. Subject searching, however, is another story.

By Subject

Before searching for a book by subject, it is helpful to have a clear idea of your topic. As discussed in chapter 1, you'll wander aimlessly if you don't know where you're going; while your topic may evolve as you proceed, you do need to have some sense of direction.

Let's say you were doing a paper on eating disorders. Your first inclination would probably be to enter the subject heading **Eating disorders**. If you do this, you will certainly find books (if your library has any on the topic). You will probably see subject headings listed on the screen similar to those in Figure 2.2.

In this example, eleven books have been located on the general topic of eating disorders. However, the three lines below this main heading—**Anorexia nervosa**, **Bulimia**, and **Compulsive eating**—offer what are known as *cross-references*. Cross-references are often narrower topics that fall under the main subject area, but they also can stand alone. By you selecting the appropriate line number, you can perform a separate search for these headings.

Below the cross-references are subheadings; these are also narrower topics under the main heading, but they subdivide

```
You searched SUBJECT for: eating disorders
        TITLES  SEARCH RESULTS       HEADINGS 1 - 9
1       [11]    Eating disorders.
2               RELATED TERM: Anorexia nervosa.
3               RELATED TERM: Bulimia.
4               RELATED TERM: Compulsive eating.
5       [1]     Eating disorders -- Bibliography.
6       [1]     Eating disorders -- Encyclopedias.
7       [1]     Eating disorders -- Etiology.
8       [1]     Eating disorders -- Etiology -- Political
                aspects.
9       [1]     Eating disorders -- Etiology -- Social aspects.
```

Figure 2.2: A typical online catalog subject display

the main heading and cannot stand alone. **Eating disorders—Bibliography** and **Eating disorders—Encyclopedias** denote specific types of books; **Eating disorders—Etiology** denotes a subdivision of the main topic (by the way, etiology, which I had to look up in the dictionary, means the study of causes), which is further subdivided into political and social aspects.

Once you have found the appropriate subject heading, you are not done, of course. You must delve a little deeper to find the individual records. In this particular example, you select the line number pertaining to the subject heading you desire (with online catalogs available through the World Wide Web, you simply *"click"* on a subject heading); this brings up a list of the individual books and other items (see Figure 2.3).

This screen gives you some basic information on the item (author, title, publisher, and year), but the final step is to choose a particular item in order to get the full record similar to that displayed in Figure 2.1. This record includes the all-important call number, which is required to actually locate the item.

```
1    Abraham, Suzanne.  Eating disorders:  the facts.  2nd ed.
     Oxford, New York: Oxford University Press.  1987.

2    Abraham, Suzanne.  Eating disorders:  the facts.  3rd ed.
     Oxford, New York: Oxford University Press.  1992.

3    Adar, Yeudith.  A short term expressive therapy support
     group for compulsive overeaters  [microform]  1991.

4    Anorexia and bulimia [videorecording].  Princeton, N.J.
     Films for the Humanities and Sciences [distributor].  1987.

5    Cernin, Kim.  The hungry self women, eating, and identity.
     1st HarperPerennial ed.  New York: HarperPerennial.  1994.
```

Figure 2.3: A typical online catalog title display

Problems with Subject Searching

Subject searching doesn't always work as smoothly as the previous example might suggest. Sure, **Eating disorders** is a subject heading, but not everything you might think to enter is going to be a heading. This is because subject headings are determined by the Library of Congress, which puts together the official list of standard, acceptable headings under which all books are categorized. The list is actually quite long, occupying the space of four large red volumes known as *The Library of Congress Subject Headings*, or, simply, the "red books."

If you don't mind leafing through the pages of these heavy red volumes, they can help you determine appropriate headings to enter in the online catalog. In this alphabetically arranged list, official headings are indicated by bold type. **Television advertising** is one such heading. If you looked up television commercials, however, it would not be in bold, and you would be instructed to "USE Television advertising." In addition, the red books also suggest headings you might not have considered. Under **Television advertising,** for example, you will find broader terms (BTs) like **Broadcast advertising,** narrower terms (NTs) like **Singing commercials,** and related terms (RTs) like **Television commercial films.** Beneath all of this, finally, will be the subheadings you can use with the main heading, such as **Television advertising—Awards.**

But it is not essential to use the Library of Congress subject heading list. The online catalog will often refer you to the official heading as well as associated headings. Let's say you were looking for books about the Vietnam War. You'd probably just enter the subject heading **Vietnam War.** Having done this, however, you would probably see the following type of message:

Vietnam War, 1961–1975 search for
Vietnamese Conflict, 1961–1975

Although this cross-reference is helpful, it does seem a bit odd that the official heading is **Vietnamese Conflict,** but it's not that surprising when you remember that the Library of Congress is a part of that quirky bureaucracy known as the U.S. Government; since the Vietnam War was never officially recognized as a war, this is not an acceptable subject heading. But when was the last time you heard someone refer to the "Vietnamese Conflict"? Just out of curiosity, I searched all the books in the library where I work to find out how many have "Vietnamese Conflict" in the title. I found none. In this same library, however, were forty-four books with "Vietnam War" in their titles. On this same issue of quirky subject headings, you'll notice that there is an apparent lack of political correctness. For example, **Indians of North America** is the official heading for Native Americans.

The wheels of the Library of Congress, as with any bureaucratic institution, move slowly. It was only a few years ago that the heading **Motion pictures** was still **Moving pic-**

ture plays. You are less likely to find terms in current usage established as subject headings. **Generation X** was just recently added to the list; before that you had to use the heading **Baby busters**. When I began writing this book and entered the term **Prozac**, I found absolutely nothing, not even a cross-reference; as of July 1996, however, even though **Prozac** was still not an official heading, I did find a cross-reference to the generic name of the drug **Fluoxetine**.

Sometimes, subject searching can be quite infuriating. If you wanted to locate books on television violence, which is not a subject heading, you might receive a message onscreen such as "Your search for a subject did not locate any titles in the database" or something to that effect. Often, just changing the word order or playing around with the phrase a bit will do the trick. For example, you will find that **Violence in television** is a valid heading.

Another suggestion is to think of synonyms for your heading. Perhaps, considering the formality of Library of Congress subject headings, you might think to enter **Daytime dramas** to find books on soap operas, when, in fact, the official heading *is* **Soap operas** despite the colloquial sound of it.

Besides referring to the *Library of Congress Subject Headings* or playing a trial-and-error game with subject searching on the online catalog, there is another way to find material. This easy method, called keyword searching, is made possible by the computerization of library catalogs.

By Keyword

Picture the old card catalog (if you can remember it). Imagine that in the drawers are filed cards not just under every author, title, and subject heading but also under each and every word in the titles, the authors' names, and the subject headings. In addition, summaries and other notes have been added for each book, and cards are also filed under each word in these summaries and notes. The card catalog would be bigger than the whole library and a bit unwieldy to use, but it would serve an essential purpose.

Suppose you were looking for books about headhunters (the kind that can get you a job, not the kind you often see on reruns of *Gilligan's Island*). If you were to pull out the appropriate "H" drawer in this massive card catalog, you would find cards for books about both varieties of headhunters. But *My Friends, the New Guinea Headhunters* by Benjamin T. Butcher certainly won't serve your research purpose. Before this, however, is a card for *How to Answer a Headhunter's Call: A Complete Guide to Executive Search* because the word "headhunter" is in the title. Since the subject heading under which this book is officially categorized is **Executives—recruiting**, doing a traditional subject search would never have located it, but this keyword searching does. This is the sort of thing that you can do with an online catalog or just about any other searchable electronic database.

A *keyword* is any word that appears in a computerized item record, except for common prepositions and articles such as *the, of, to,* and the like which are called stopwords. A keyword could be in the title field, the subject field, the notes field—any field. You can search for single words or phrases, as well as combinations of words or phrases.

It's a good idea to take a look at the subject headings of the records you find through keyword searching because, depending on how many books you need, you may want to do a traditional subject search using some of these headings. Keyword searching doesn't always find every book. For example, if you look up **daytime drama** as a keyword phrase, you'll only find the records that contain this phrase. Replace with these records will all list *Soap Operas* as a subject heading. Not every record for books on soap operas, however, will contain the phrase **daytime drama**. If you return to traditional subject searching and look up **Soap operas**, you will get a complete list of all the books on this topic.

Using the Connector "and"

The real power of keyword searching is demonstrated when you need to look up more than one word or phrase. For example, let's say you can't remember the exact title of a book, but you know that some guy named Peter wrote a really great book about the stock market, and you think Wall Street might be in the title. Through the magic of computers you could find Peter Lynch's *One Up on Wall Street* by entering the keyword search: **peter and wall street**. Isn't that neat! What you've told the computer to do is to find all the records that contain both the name **Peter** and the phrase **Wall Street**.

Boolean Logic

Keyword searching using more than one term or phrase such as in the previous example operates according to the principles of Boolean Logic, which were developed by George Boole, a nineteenth-century mathematician. But don't worry if you're not good with math because it really doesn't involve calculating numbers; the computer does all that work. Boolean Logic can be used to define a topic very specifically, so that from among millions of items in a library you can find the ones that meet your needs. The principles I'll discuss here are extremely important because they form the basis of searching any computerized database, not just an online catalog.

Suppose you wanted books about drug abuse among women. To understand Boolean Logic, picture two sets of books: the first contains all the books about women, and the second contains all the books about drug abuse. A third set is formed by the books that belong in both sets because they're about both women and drug abuse. When the linking term *and* is used, records that contain the two words specified are retrieved. Figure 2.4 illustrates what is going on.

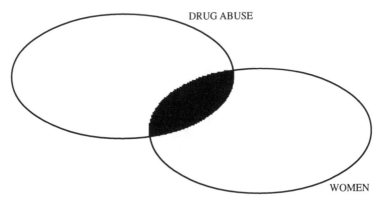

Figure 2.4: Diagram representing a search for
women and drug abuse.

The portion of this diagram in black is the set representing records that include the terms **women** and **drug abuse**.
The more terms you link together, the narrower your search
becomes and the fewer records you will retrieve. For instance a search for **women and drug abuse and treatment**
will retrieve a narrower set, as in Figure 2.5.

The portion of this diagram in black is the set representing records that include the terms **women** and **drug abuse**
and **treatment**. Notice that it is smaller than the highlighted
portion in Figure 2.4.

If you don't find any books or if you only find a few, you
can try dropping a term. This will broaden your search. Or
if you get too much, narrow your search by adding a term.
You will find that keyword searching can often be a process
of trial and error.

Using the Connector "or"

You can also use the word *or* between terms to broaden a
search when keyword searching. Picture a set containing all
the books about air pollution and another set containing all
the books about water pollution. Some of these books may
certainly overlap in subject material covering both topics.

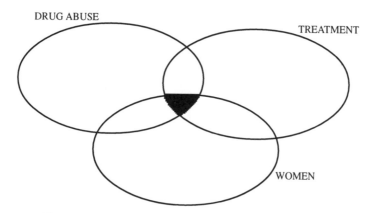

DRUG ABUSE

TREATMENT

WOMEN

Figure 2.5: Diagram representing a search for **women
and drug abuse and treatment**.

But the set resulting from a search for **air pollution or water pollution** will contain not only the books that address
both topics but also those that are about one or the other.

In Figure 2.6, the area in black represents those books that
address both topics, but the areas in gray are also included
in the resultant set because the connecting term *or* was used.
If you were to add another term to this search using *or*, the
outcome would be even larger because the more terms you
link together with *or*, the broader your search becomes; this
is the opposite of what happens when using *and*.

Or is also useful when you want to enter synonyms for a
word so you don't miss any pertinent material—for example,
motion pictures or movies or films. In addition, you can
use it if you're not sure of the spelling of a name or word
(**smith or smythe**) or to retrieve variant spellings of a word
(**theatre or theater**).

Truncation

Truncation can serve a similar purpose. With this technique,
you drop the ending of a word and replace it with a truncation symbol. This symbol differs among online catalogs; the

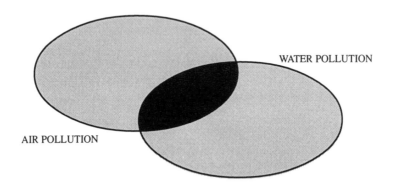

Figure 2.6: Diagram representing a search for **air pollution or water pollution**.

question mark (?), asterisk (*), and pound sigs (#) are frequently used. For example, you could enter **environment?**, which would retrieve all of the records containing any words beginning with environment; in addition to environment, you would retrieve environments, environmental, environmentalists, and so on.

Truncation is also helpful when you want to retrieve both the plural and singular forms of a word; just substitute the catalog's truncation symbol for the **s**. You can also use truncation symbols within words to act like a wild card. For instance, if you wanted to find either **woman** or **women**, you could enter **wom?n**, which would serve the same purpose as **woman or women**.

Truncation is not limited to searching online catalogs. You can use it in just about any searchable electronic database.

Using the Connector "not"

You can use the word *not* between terms to eliminate irrelevant items. For example, if you wanted to find all the books about drug abuse except those dealing with alcohol abuse,

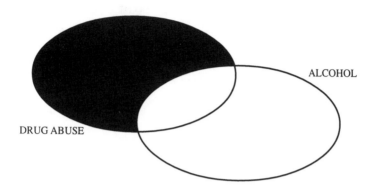

Figure 2.7: Diagram representing a search for **drug abuse not alcohol**.

you could enter the search as **drug abuse not alcohol**. This would eliminate all the records in which the word alcohol appears, as Figure 2.7 illustrates.

In this figure, the resultant set is again represented by the area in black, but it is not a part of both original sets, only the set of books about drug abuse. Although *not* is used less often than the other two connecting terms, it can be very helpful in avoiding one of the pitfalls of keyword searching—retrieving irrelevant records.

Combining Connecting Terms

You can combine the *and, or,* and *not* in one search to get really specific. Usually this involves throwing in some parentheses so the computer doesn't get confused. For example, **(drug abuse not alcohol) and women** will retrieve records concerning drug abuse among women but not alcohol abuse. **Children and violence and (motion pictures or television)** will retrieve books about the effects of television or motion picture violence upon children.

Using parentheses when combining sets in this way is necessary to define your search criteria clearly to the dumb computer. The parentheses separate the parts of the search having different connecting terms. The part of the search in parentheses will be performed first. Whatever set of records results from this initial search will then be combined with the rest of the search statement. (Note that in some computerized databases, instead of using parentheses, you just perform separate searches for each part of your topic and then combine your results; this achieves the same results as using parentheses.)

Figuring out where to put the parentheses is generally just a process of determining what makes sense. If I searched for **drug abuse not (alcohol and women)** instead of **(drug abuse not alcohol) and women**, I wouldn't find any books on women because the *not* eliminates both words inside the parentheses. **(Children and violence and motion pictures) or television** will retrieve books about children and motion picture violence as well as every book in the library about television. If you misplace your parentheses, you may just get a message to the effect that the computer doesn't understand what you want. Just experiment. You'll get the feel for this technique after you've tried it out a bit.

Problems with Keyword Searching

Nothing is perfect. Although keyword searching offers solutions to the problems of subject searching, it does have problems all its own. As already mentioned, keyword searching does not retrieve every record on a certain subject. That is why it is important to also return to subject searching if you need more material. Keyword searching also retrieves irrelevant records because it often takes words out of context. If you wanted a book about the architecture of Boston and were to enter **boston and architecture**, in addition to retrieving all the records for books about Boston architecture, you would also retrieve all the books about architecture that were published in Boston but not necessarily about Boston. Keywords, remember, are picked up from all fields—including the publisher.

There is a more complex level of keyword searching that lets you specify the particular fields in which you want to search. In some systems you place **su** before the term, which directs the computer to look for the term in the subject field only. So if you entered the more specific search **su boston and su architecture** or **su (boston and architecture)**, which accomplishes the same thing, you would eliminate the irrelevant books. I will discuss this technique, known as field specific searching, in greater detail in chapter 7.

TAKE THE ONLINE CATALOG FOR A SPIN

Now that I've given you the keys to using the online catalog, take it for a spin. The best way to really learn anything, after all, is by doing. At first it may be a little strange and difficult, and you'll really have to concentrate on what you're doing, but after a while it will become second nature. Remember when you first sat in the driver's seat. I recall wondering how I would ever be able to hold a conversation while driving. I had to focus intently on what I was doing; it was all very nerve-wracking. But now I can drive while drinking coffee, singing along with the radio, and putting together a shopping list in my head.

Three

Traveling through the Stacks

T he first time I went into New York City by myself I felt a bit anxious. I was afraid I wouldn't find my friends, whom I had planned to meet near Macy's. But my anxiety was a bit unjustified because, despite the immensity of Manhattan, it's really very easy to find your way around. Whoever originally designed the road system laid out most of the streets in a gridlike pattern. So instead of all the streets being uniquely named, most were simply numbered. This makes it possible to determine if you're going in the right direction even if you've never been there before.

I had to get to Fifth Avenue and 34th Street from the Port Authority bus station, which I easily determined upon exiting was at Eighth Avenue and 42nd Street. This is not the nicest area, by the way, so I was hesitant to ask for directions. I just started walking down Eighth Avenue and the next block happened to be 43rd Street, so I knew I was going in the wrong direction. I turned around. When I reached 34th Street, I took a left, which just happened to be the correct choice this time, because the next street I came to was Seventh Avenue. Going two blocks further, I reached my destination.

Libraries are a lot like Manhattan. Although usually a bit quieter, libraries can be big and often overwhelming. When people go into them, they often think it will be hard to find their way around. Libraries these days certainly contain much more than just books, but books still take up the most space, and books are often what you look for when you begin your research. The average college library contains hundreds of thousands of books; a large university library contains millions! But you can easily find what you need amid this overwhelming amount of material if you understand how all these books are organized.

THE LAY OF THE LAND

There really weren't too many libraries around before the nineteenth century, except for those catering to the needs of academic institutions and individuals who could afford to pay dues. Each one of these private libraries organized its books in a different way. But in the 1800s, several factors all related to the Industrial Revolution led to the rise of libraries. A more technologically literate society was needed to support the rise of industry, so public education and literacy became widespread. At the same time, technological advances in printing, which transformed it from a manual to a mechanical process, made the production of books less expensive and easier. Finally, Andrew Carnegie and other leaders of industry donated large sums of money to support the building of new libraries. With more books, more people reading them, and more libraries, there was a greater need for a standard system of organization. Two systems actually emerged: the Dewey Decimal Classification used in many public libraries and some smaller college libraries; and the Library of Congress (LC) Classification, the standard in larger public institutions and most academic libraries.

If you want to be able to find your way around the library without going crazy, you need to be familiar with either the Library of Congress system or, less frequently, Dewey Decimals, depending on which is used by your library. Students constantly come to me for help because they can't find a book, and in many cases this is simply because they don't really understand the system that is used to arrange them. There are probably countless other students who don't ask for directions and instead just wander through the stacks wasting precious time and getting frustrated. To avoid getting lost in the stacks, here's a crash course in what is called *classification*.

Every book in a library is given a unique number—a *call number*—to indicate its location. You find out a book's call number by looking it up in the library's online catalog. With Dewey Decimals as well as the LC Classification, the subject matter and the author's name determine the number a book is given, which in turn determines its location on the shelf.

The Dewey Decimal Classification

The Dewey Decimal Classification divides knowledge down into ten broad categories from 000 through the 900s (see Table 3.1). Each broad category is subdivided into ten more sections, which are each further subdivided into ten smaller sections and so on until you get down to the level of individual books that will have call numbers involving decimals. For example, if you are interested in literature, the books you want are located between 800 and 899. More specifically, books of American literature are between 810 and 819. This is further subdivided into sections such as poetry, drama, and essays, each designated by a whole number. Nineteenth-century American writers are found within the 818 section. A copy of Henry David Thoreau's classic *Walden* has the specific call number 818.31.

The part of the number following the decimal point can be a bit confusing, especially if you never really got a grip on decimals in math class. Just to clarify, decimals don't have the same value as whole numbers. For instance, *Walden* as well as books about *Walden* at 818.31 will actually be found after a book with a number like 818.2987, because .31

Table 3.1 Dewey Decimal Classification

000–099   **General works**—like encyclopedias, but a lot of other topics have been thrown in over the years ranging from Bigfoot and UFOs to computers.

100–199   **Philosophy**—this also includes psychology, astrology, witchcraft, and other related topics.

200–299   **Religion**—200–289 includes Christianity, while all other world religions are crammed into the 290–299 section.

300–399   **Social science**—includes sociology, political science, economics, law, education, and related topics.

400–499   **Languages**—here you will find books about individual languages as well as linguistics in general.

500–599   **Natural sciences** (as opposed to applied sciences, which are covered in the next section)—books on mathematics, astronomy, chemistry, physics, and life sciences are found here.

600–699   **Technology**—includes applied sciences such as medicine, engineering, and cooking.

700–799   **Fine arts**—includes painting, sculpture, music, performing arts, television, games, and the like.

800–899   **Literature**—includes classic literary works as well as literary criticism, but does not usually include contemporary fiction and other works not considered "classic" (these are generally kept in a separate fiction section arranged by author).

900–999   **History**—in addition to historical topics, includes biographies which are all kept in the 920 section.

is more than .2987. When using decimals, zeros get dropped, so .31 is really the same as .310 or .3100 and so on to infinity. When the zeroes are appended, it's easier to see that .3100 is greater than .2987.

The Dewey Decimal Classification has some inherent weaknesses. Its hierarchical scheme has a strong bias toward western culture as well as a lack of concern for what we refer to today as "political correctness." A similar situation is obvious with the emphasis on American, English, and European literatures. Between 800 and 889 are found all the books by and about American, British, and Western European literature. The literature of countries that were considered alien to most people in nineteenth-century America—Asian, African, and Middle Eastern countries as well as Russia, Poland, and many others—is squeezed between 890 and 899.

Another problem with this system is that, as new subjects arise, they must be shoehorned in somewhere; the original nineteenth-century scheme had no place for topics such as computer programming and soap operas. Computer books have been thrown in with the encyclopedias, and you'll find the books about soap operas along with all the other books on television and movies in the fine arts section, specifically 791.4 (not even a whole number!). Because of this, books in these and other unforeseen areas must have long and complicated call numbers in order to give each a unique location.

The Library of Congress Classification

The Library of Congress Classification is more complex. It is used by some larger public libraries, many academic libraries, and, of course, by the Library of Congress, which designed it in the nineteenth century to organize the increasing number of books in its collection. This national library has grown from a small, one-room, legal collection established in the Capitol in 1802 for the use of Congress to a massive institution that contains over one hundred million items. Such a vast collection requires a specific scheme of organization; Dewey Decimals just don't hack it.

The LC Classification breaks all of knowledge down into twenty broad categories indicated by letters of the alphabet (see Table 3.2). You'll find encyclopedias in the A section, atlases in the G section, and literature in the P section. These basic categories are subdivided alphabetically. For example, while books on literature in general are given the letter P, English literature is PR, and American literature is PS.

The LC system is alphanumeric. Following the initial one, two, or, occasionally, three-letter code are numbers that further divide a particular topic. If you're looking for humor (which you may be needing if you've gotten this far in the chapter), go to the PN6160s. A particular book like Jerry Seinfeld's *Sein Language* has the call number PN6162 .S358. Locating this book on the shelf is akin to locating Fifth Avenue and 34th Street in Manhattan, since the books are all shelved in a certain order. But the Library of Congress system is more complicated than this analogy implies because, like the Dewey Decimal Classification, it also utilizes decimal points as well as an often confusing jumble of letters and numbers. It's more like having to get to Macy's, find the shoe department, and select a pair of shoes in your size.

Let's say you want to get *Sein Language* at PN6162 .S358. First, you have to find out where the P section is located by consulting a floor chart or by asking your friendly librarian who will be much more approachable than many of the characters you'll find in the Port Authority bus terminal. Once you find the general P section, finding the PNs is simply a matter of alphabetical order—they'll be somewhere between PM and PO. When you find the PNs, follow the call numbers numerically until you get to 6162. Don't confuse this with the Dewey system and look for 616.2. If you try looking for PN616.2, you'll wind up in a totally different section from PN6162 and see lots of books

Table 3.2 Library of Congress Classification

A **General works** such as encyclopedias.

B **Philosophy, religion,** and **psychology.**

C **History**—special topics like archaeology, genealogy, and general biography.

D **World history.**

E/F **American** and **Canadian history.**

G **Geography** (mostly)—in addition to atlases and books about various geographic areas, you'll also find books about the environment, dancing, and sports.

H **Social sciences**—includes sociology, economics, and business.

J **Political sciences.**

K **Law.**

L **Education.**

M **Music.**

N **Fine arts**—includes painting, sculpture, and architecture.

P **Literature**—also includes theater, movies, and television.

Q **Natural sciences**—mathematics, astronomy, chemistry, physics, life sciences, and so on.

R **Medicine.**

S **Agriculture.**

T **Technology**—other applied sciences like engineering, photography, and cooking.

U **Military science.**

V **Naval science.**

Z **Bibliography**—library science as well as bibliographies that list materials on various subjects.

about classical, medieval, and renaissance literature (not exactly the area I go to for kicks).

Now, in continuing your search for PN6162 .S358, you switch back to the alphabet to find S (which stands for Jerry's last name). Once you've done that, you encounter the trickiest part of the LC Classification: the dreaded decimals. You need to look for .358 (just drop the S now that you've found it). Recalling our discussion of decimals earlier in the chapter, would *Sein Language* at PN6162 .S358 be found before or after *You Have a Hang-up If...*by Marcia Seligson, Mort Gerberg, and Avery Corman at PN6162 .S37? Is .358 greater than .37? No, because .37 is the same as .370, which is obviously greater than .358. What about a book called *Copycat* by Barbara Samuels at PN6162 .S2513? If you've got a grip on decimals now, you'll have no problem determining that it will be found before *Sein Language*. To make sure this is all clear, let me list the order in which you'd find the books:

PN6162 .S2513	*Copycat*
PN6162 .S358	*Sein Language*
PN6162 .S37	*You Have a Hang-up If...*

At first glance, you might have thought that these books would actually go in the opposite order, but if you just insert some mental zeros, it becomes clear that this is the proper arrangement. The year of publication is often included at the end of the call number, but I have omitted that above so the numbers appear a bit less daunting. This date is only important in distinguishing one edition of a book from another.

Although I've gotten into some picky details here, what often happens in reality is that you find the general section you need such as PN6162 and then, realizing that the books in this section are arranged by the author's last name, simply scan the titles on the shelf to find what you need rather than straining your eyes looking at those little call numbers on the book spines. This can work effectively in many situations.

Library of Congress call numbers, however, are not always as simple as in the humor section. I mentioned before that when classification systems were developed in the nineteenth century, many subjects did not even exist. So when books about airplanes, television, and break dancing were written, they had to be fit in somewhere. As a result, what has happened is that a lot of books have been crammed into very small call number ranges and therefore must have very long call numbers with lots of digits and decimals.

For example, let's take a look at the section of the library that contains books about the Internet. Although just a few years ago there were no books about the Internet, now there are hundreds, and all of them are designated by the general call number TK5105.875 .I57. A particular book like *The Complete Idiot's Pocket Reference to the Internet* by Neal Goldman has the lengthy call number TK5105.875 .I57 G65.

If you break down the call number TK5105.875 .I57 G65, it's really not too much harder to find than *Sein Language*; it just looks more intimidating. After finding TK and 5105, you look for .875 the way you look for any decimal. Then you find .I57 by first locating the Is and then .57. Finally, after finding G, you regard 65 as a decimal also even though there's no decimal point before the G. In the LC scheme, any number after the initial whole number is regarded as a decimal. So *The Internet for Windows* by David C. Gardner at TK5105.875 .I57 G368 will be found before TK5105.875 .I57 G65.

There is another confusing aspect of the LC classification. Where's the fiction section? Libraries that use LC numbers don't have a separate fiction section as do public libraries using Dewey Decimals. This is because the LC scheme is intended more for research than for recreational purposes. All fiction is put in the literature section (designated by call numbers beginning with P), side by side with criticism of the various works. The same is true for biographical material; whereas Dewey libraries put all biographies in the 920s, LC libraries have them scattered throughout the collection depending on the occupation of the person about whom the book is written.

Once you get familiar with the system used to organize books, you can do some "educated browsing." Although, in chapter 1, I said that browsing is not an effective way to do research, if you practice what we could call "educated browsing" in a certain call number area, you can often find some useful material. Of course, if you're looking for something really narrow, you may have problems. Restrict your browsing to more general information on a topic. To be an "educated browser," look up your subject in the online catalog and find a few relevant books and their call numbers. Then, after locating these books in the stacks, take a look at what other books are on the shelf.

Another way to find further material once you're in the stacks and have found a few books is to look in the back of each of these books for a bibliography of sources. If you notice any titles in the bibliography that look pertinent, look them up in the online catalog to see if your library has them. Since book authors also may use periodical articles as sources for their books, titles of these articles may be listed in the bibliography.

Many books are hard to classify because they might involve more than one subject. A book about the psychology of women, for example, may be classified in the HQ section rather than BF, which is the primary psychology section, because HQ contains books on women's studies. Depending on how you look at the book, it could fit in either section. If this book on the psychology of women was of a medical nature, it could be placed in the RCs. If there's only one copy of the book, however, it can only have one distinct call number. This same problem can occur when a book is classified with the Dewey Decimal system. This is why it is important to use the online catalog rather than just meander through the stacks because you may find that books on basically the same subject are scattered through different call number areas.

I mentioned that both the Library of Congress and Dewey Decimal Classifications were developed as indirect responses to the Industrial Revolution. As we undergo another period of change, the Information Revolution, these two systems, despite their quirks, still serve to give some order to what could easily be chaos. With the knowledge you now posess about both systems, finding the books that you need won't be as complicated as initially it might have seemed. The important thing to remember is to just take it one step at a time. Breaking down anything into smaller parts makes it easier to deal with, whether it be researching and writing your term paper, locating a book in the stacks, or making your way through the streets of Manhattan.

Four

Sight-Seeing in the Reference Room

I magine driving through the Sahara desert, an arid waste-
land that comprises a large portion of northern Africa,
without provisions or even a map. Before long, you'd
need to find water to survive and gas to get you out of there.
But how would you find these things? You'd probably just
have to wander around and hope for the best.

This situation is very similar to completing a library "scavenger hunt," a frustrating type of assignment often given by
professors who believe that, by wandering around the Reference Room looking for the answers to a list of trivial and
unrelated questions, you will learn a lot about the library.
More likely, you will become discouraged because you won't
have a clue about where to find the answers. In fact, after
completing a scavenger hunt you may never want to come
back to the library again. Sure, if you were having trouble,
you could go to a librarian for help with answering a specific question, but then you really wouldn't learn very much
from the experience, because by that point you'd probably
just want to get the assignment done and get out of there.

I think a more effective way to learn about the typical
Reference Room of an academic library is for me to give
you a figurative road map by guiding you through it first and
pointing out the major "sights" that are the basic types of
reference sources that will be most useful for your research.
In this chapter, I'll pose some trivial (yet fascinating) ques-

41

tions; then, I'll show you how you can find the answers effectively using some helpful sources, so if you encounter a similar question in the future, you'll know what sources to use.

Before I begin the "tour," we should first consider the increasing variety of reference sources that are becoming available in computerized formats, either on CD-ROM or online. Electronic encyclopedias are a popular type of computerized reference source. *The New Grolier Multimedia Encyclopedia*, for example—a CD-ROM version of the *Academic American Encyclopedia*—is a best-seller; and *Britannica Online*, the computerized version of *Encyclopedia Britannica*, can now be accessed on the World Wide Web if your library subscribes to this service. Although in this chapter I may focus on the book versions of these reference sources, you can check in your library to see if a particular title is available through a computer. Despite the difference in formats between print and computer, however, the content remains basically the same. Therefore, being familiar with the sources discussed in this chapter will prove valuable no matter how you actually access the source.

No college library will have every source mentioned here, but a good library will have a large percentage of them, as well as many other titles that fall into the general categories of reference material described in this chapter. A library's reference book collection is usually organized according to the same classification scheme used to arrange circulating books, and records for these reference books should be included in the online catalog.

WHERE SHOULD I START? ENCYCLOPEDIAS

Q: Where did the potato originate?

A: Although it is considered a staple of the Irish diet, so much so that the failure of the potato crop in 1846 led to widespread famine, the common potato did not originate in Ireland. It is actually indigenous to the Andes mountains in South America, where it was enjoyed by the ancient Incans. The potato was only introduced to Europe in the sixteenth century after Spanish explorers returned from their voyages of discovery with this treasure.

Source: *Academic American Encyclopedia* [1].

Encyclopedias, whether computerized or in their traditional place upon the bookshelves, are often a good place to start your research because they provide concise, factual overviews on a vast number of subjects. Encyclopedias are probably one of the first things that come to mind when you hear the term "reference books." You should find the volumes of general encyclopedias like *Britannica, Collier's,* and *Americana* in the **A** call number section of the Reference Room, along with other general works.

If you were writing a research paper on the social significance of the potato, you would find a short essay on this versatile vegetable in the **P** volume of the *Academic American Encyclopedia.* As the next question demonstrates, however, it's not always so easy to find information in the print (meaning noncomputerized) version of an encyclopedia.

Stopping for Directions: Consulting the Index

Q: Who were the *Plastic People of the Universe?*

A: No, they weren't Saturday morning television cartoon characters. This was the name of a Czechoslovakian band whose members were arrested in the mid-1970s along with other intellectuals, artists, and students who belonged to the Charter 77 movement, which protested the repressive measures imposed after the Soviet invasion. The band's arrest motivated the playwright Vaclav Havel and others to sign a manifesto demanding respect for human and civil rights.

Source: *Encyclopedia Americana* [2].

The answer to this question is in the **C** volume of *Ency-clopedia Americana,* not the **P** volume. If your subject is not in the appropriate lettered volume, it's probably not broad enough to have its own entry in a general encyclopedia. So you can look it up in the index, which is usually the final volume of the set. In this case, *Plastic People of the Universe* is in volume 8 (the **C** volume) under the heading **Czechoslovakia**.

The index is also handy because you can locate all the entries relating to your topic, not just the one that starts with a particular first letter. For instance, if you look up **World War II** in the index volume of any general encyclopedia, you'll be referred to a number of subtopics in different volumes that all relate to the main topic. This will give you more information than would be contained in the **W** volume alone.

I will be mentioning indexes many times in the following pages, because they are really the key to using the book versions of most reference sources, and are also helpful in finding information in many nonfiction books in the circulating collection. If you're having trouble finding the information that you need in a particular source, chances are there is an alphabetical index either in the back of a one-volume source, or in the final volume of a multivolume set (like a general encyclopedia) that will indicate on which page to locate your information.

Electronic versions of reference books do not utilize indexes, because computerized sources obviously don't have page numbers. The advantage of using an electronic encyclopedia or any other CD-ROM or online reference source is that you can search it more easily by entering keywords. But since, in reality, most reference books have not been computerized, using the indexes provided in these books is often essential.

Off the Main Drag: Subject-Specific Encyclopedias

Q: How did the mood ring, that short lived jewelry fad of the 1970s really work? And why did Sophia Loren's mood ring make tabloid headlines in 1975?

A: Inside the stone of the mood ring were heat-sensitive liquid crystals derived through a chemical process from sheep's wool, the same stuff that had been used for years in hospital thermometers. In 1975, Sophia Loren stopped a press conference because to her horror her mood ring had turned black—a very bad omen!

Source: *The Encyclopedia of Bad Taste.*[3]

I couldn't find any entries for *mood rings* in traditional general encyclopedias, and I checked four different ones. This is where subject-specific encyclopedias sometimes come in handy. The subjects covered by the *Encyclopedia of Bad Taste* include a variety of atrocious fads of the 1970s such as mood rings, disco, and bell bottoms as well as the short-lived phenomena of other decades.

Whereas each major general encyclopedia consists of many volumes, specialized encyclopedias are often just one volume, although many are also multivolume sets. Besides finding topics that may not be covered in general encyclopedias, these specialized books can go into much greater depth. More common specialized encyclopedias include the *Encyclopedia of Philosophy*, the *Encyclopedia of Religion*, and the *Encyclopedia of American Social History*. But in addition to the *Encyclopedia of Bad Taste*, you might also find such off-beat titles as the *Star Trek Encyclopedia* and the *Encyclopedia of Unbelief*. Ask a librarian if there is an appropriate encyclopedia that focuses on your topic area. Or, if you're feeling really clever, try a keyword search in the online catalog. For example, if you want to find out if there is an encyclopedia about sleep enter **encyclopedias and sleep**.

WHAT DOES IT MEAN? DICTIONARIES

Q: What are the following: (1) phrenophobia, (2) soogee-moogee, and (3) the best boy?

A: (1) *Phrenophobia* is a "morbid fear of having to think, endemic to politicians, or a morbid fear of losing one's mind." (common also to many college students).

(2) *Soogie-moogee* is a slang term for a "mixture containing soda used for cleaning paintwork and woodwork on boats" (not to be confused with sudzy-dudzy or squeegie-weegie).

(3) If you've ever sat through the closing credits of a movie, like I have on a few occasions when the movie was really good, you've probably wondered what the *best boy* does. Basically, the best boy is the chief assistant to the gaffer (the chief electrician) on a motion picture set.

Sources: (1) *The International Dictionary of Psychology.*[4]
(2) *The Oxford Dictionary of Modern Slang.*[5]
(3) *The Complete Film Dictionary.*[6]

Aside from the usual language dictionaries you may consult from time to time like *American Heritage* and *Webster's*, there are numerous specialized dictionaries such as those mentioned above. You could also consider them mini-encyclopedias providing in an alphabetical format brief definitions of terms used in a particular field of study. In fact, sometimes it's hard to draw the line between encyclopedias and dictionaries. The basic difference is in the length of the entries; a dictionary implies brief definitions, while an encyclopedia contains lengthier essays.

WHICH SIDE SHOULD I TAKE? RESEARCHING "HOT" TOPICS

Q: Should drugs be legalized?

A: Yes and no, obviously, depending on who you ask. There is no straightforward answer to this question. For example, Ethan Nadelmann, a political science professor at Princeton, favors drug legalization because the current prohibition policy is too costly and ineffective. David Courtwright, who teaches history at the University of North Florida, argues that since drug legalization would not extend to minors, a black market would continue.

Source: *CQ Researcher.*[7]

The material collected in *CQ Researcher* covers a veritable encyclopedia's breadth of controversial issues. If you're writing a paper about some hot topic such as the legalization of drugs, gun control, or abortion, this is an excellent source. Published by Congressional Quarterly in Washington, DC, each annual volume consists of forty-eight well-researched reports; each takes a broad look at a subject of current interest. The reports follow the same general format; in addition to a brief overview of the subject, there are also such features as a chronology of events relating to the topic, a pro–con argument on a particular question such as that asked above, and a bibliography of further resources to check and organizations to contact. Older volumes published before 1991 go by the title *Editorial Research Reports.* You may have access to *CQ Researcher* in a computerized format, since a CD-ROM version is now available.

Q: What was the general response of newspapers to the admission of a female, Shannon Faulkner, to the Citadel military college in South Carolina in 1994?

A: Most of the nation's leading papers were obsessed with discussing the court-ordered shaving of Faulkner's head, as reflected in these assorted comments:

> Faulkner may not agree with the practice [of head shaving]. But if she wants to truly belong at the Citadel, she can't buy just part of the program. (*Rockford Register Star*, 8/14/94)

> It constitutes an unnecessary indignity. (*The Christian Science Monitor*, 8/5/94)

> Are the clippers that await Shannon Faulkner an instrument of sexist spite, or the means to the very equality she sought by challenging the Citadel's all-male composition in court? In truth, they are both. (*Pittsburgh Post Gazette*, 8/13/94)

Source: *Editorials On File.*[8]

Editorials On File, which is published in twice monthly installments which are collected in a ring binder and then bound together at the end of the year, will save you a lot of time if you are researching controversial topics. It collects editorials from all the major newspapers in the United States on a wide variety of topics. Since most smaller libraries don't subscribe to many of these papers, this source gives you access to material that wouldn't otherwise be readily available. It also saves you from having to deal with microfilm.

You can find the editorials you need by using the index provided in the back of each annual volume. For instance, you could look up **Faulkner** and be referred to the appropriate page numbers in the volume, or, if you couldn't remember Faulkner's name you could also look up the **Citadel**. One catch is that it is helpful to know in what year the event happened because there is no *cumulative index*, which is an index that covers not only the particular volume you're using but also all preceding volumes. *Editorials On*

File doesn't have one, so you'd need to know this particular event occurred in 1994 or else spend a lot of time searching through a number of different volumes before finding the one you need. For the current year refer to the monthly quarterly, and semi-annual indexes provided. Another problem you may encounter with this and other indexes is difficulty in locating your subject. For example, if you look up **drugs**, you'll find no references, but if you look under **Narcotics and dangerous drugs** you will. As you can guess, using a book's index can set you off on another scavenger hunt.

HOW MUCH? HOW MANY? FINDING STATISTICAL INFORMATION

Q: Which is the more popular pet in the United States: the cat or the dog?

A: Among the entire population of the United States, the dog wins this contest when counting the actual number of households with pets; in 1991, 34.6 million households (36.5 percent) had a dog while 29.2 million households (30.9 percent) had a cat. However, the average number of dogs owned by each household was 1.5, while the average number of cats was 2, so, the actual population of pet cats in the United States was 57 million while that of dogs was 52.5 million. Cats are also more popular in single and two-person households. And so, the controversy rages on.

Source: *Statistical Abstract of the United States.*[9]

Statistical Abstract of the United States is the first place you should check for any sort of national statistical information. It is an annual collection of statistics derived from the government census as well as from private sources. Under the heading **Pet ownership/supplies** in the volume's index, you'll be referred to table 400 (not page 400). You'll often find that more than one table is cited after a heading. When you locate the appropriate tables, be sure to note the year of the information given. Just because you're using the most recent volume doesn't mean you're getting the most recent information; the pet statistics, you will note, were from 1991.

Q: What percentage of U.S. households have at least one television set? How many people in Angola "share" a television?

A: Of all U.S. households 98 percent own at least one television set (38 percent have two). In Angola, at the other extreme, there is one television set for every 210 people!

Source: *World Almanac and Book of Facts.*[10]

If you require statistics for another country, a good place to check is the *World Almanac and Book of Facts.* Although this source includes primarily U.S. information, there is a long section that contains a brief entry for each country. Other helpful sources for more in-depth international information are the *Europa World Yearbook,* the *Statesman's Yearbook*, and the *CIA World Factbook.* Many other statistical sources exist, of course, some of which are much narrower in their content, focusing on a particular geographic area or group of people.

WHAT HAPPENED? WHEN?

Q: When did Nancy Kerrigan, the 1994 Olympic silver medalist in women's figure skating, parade with Mickey Mouse through Disney World, and what did she say during this parade that tarnished her public image? On what date did she host *Saturday Night Live*?

A: The parade was on March 1, 1994, and during it, Kerrigan was heard to say, "This is so corny!" She hosted *SNL* on March 12.

Source: *Facts On File World News Digest.*[11]

Facts On File World News Digest is a news service that provides biweekly summaries of world events. These digests are collected in a binder throughout the year and then bound up into annual volumes. *Facts On File World News Digest* is also now available in a CD-ROM version that covers from 1980 on.

The key to finding information in the print volumes is to use the index that is found in the back of each one. Like *Editorials On File*, there is no cumulative index, so it is helpful to know what year you require. Since this event happened in 1994, you will find the following entry under the heading **Kerrigan, Nancy** in the index to the 1994 volume: **Disney comments aired 3–1, hosts Sat Night Live 3–12, 236E2.** From this information, you can immediately answer the part of the question concerning when the events occurred, because the dates on which events happened are included right in the index. For more information you need to go to the page number cited, which comes last in the entry (236E2). Each fact-filled page of *Facts On File* is divided into columns 1, 2, and 3, and rows A through G like a grid so you can quickly find the information you need. On page 236, if you go down to section E of column 2, you'll find the sordid details of the Disney World fiasco.

Q: In what years did the following events in motion picture history occur:

1. the first sound movie?
2. the first Academy Awards?
3. the first drive-in movie theater?
4. the first 3-D movie?
5. the first psycho-slasher film?

A: 1. 1927 (*The Jazz Singer* with Al Jolson)
     2. 1929
     3. 1933 (in New Jersey)
     4. 1953
     5. 1978 (*Halloween*)

Source: *New York Public Library Book of Chronologies.*[12]

If you need to know when an event took place, you could refer to *Facts On File World News Digest*, but remember you should know the year in order to use this source efficiently (unless you are searching the CD-ROM version). For events of a more historic and thematic nature spanning a number of years, such as motion picture history, it is better to use a chronological reference source. Aside from the source I have cited above, there are numerous such books, some covering many different historical topics, others focusing on a single theme such as major American wars or women's history.

The *New York Public Library Book of Chronologies* is an example of a thematically arranged chronology. The table of contents lists the subjects covered, including a whole section on entertainment—which points out a common method of approaching a reference book or any nonfiction book in which you need to find particular information. Although the index in the back of the book is important, sometimes all you really need to do is just look at the table of contents.

WHO? FINDING BIOGRAPHICAL INFORMATION

Q: When is Gloria Estefan's birthday, and where can I send a card?

A: September 1, 1957; send your birthday greetings to: Estefan Enterprises Inc., 6205 Bird Rd., Miami Florida 33155.

Source: *Who's Who in America.*[13]

This is just one of the many *Who's Who* books, which also include *Who Was Who in America* (for famous dead people), *Who's Who in Show Business*, *Who's Who Among Women*, and on and on. What all of these books have in common is an alphabetical format that contains very brief entries on notable people. There is usually contact information of some sort included (not in the *Who Was Who* books, obviously), and all the important dates and accomplishments in the person's life.

Q: What are Jerry Seinfeld's hobbies, and why does he never go on vacation?

A: The comedian enjoys baseball, sports cars, and expensive watches. When asked why he never takes a vacation, he replied, "From what? My whole life is a vacation."

Source: *Current Biography Yearbook.*[14]

If you want more in-depth information on a notable person, refer to *Current Biography* yearbooks or the CD-ROM version that was recently released. This series provides biographical essays on people who made an impact on the world in a particular year in some field—perhaps politics, sports, or entertainment. Each annual print volume is arranged alphabetically, so you look up a person's name in the cumulative index for 1940–1990, which will tell you the year of the volume to look in (for more recent years, see the index in the back of each individual volume); some people are included in more than one volume if they require an update. There is also an occupational index that enables you to find biographies of people in a certain profession even if you have no particular names in mind.

There are many other sources for biographical information in the typical reference collection, some of which may focus on a particular country, ethnic group, time period, or occupation. *Dictionary of American Biography*, for example, covers figures of note in American history; the *Contemporary Authors* series and the *Dictionary of Literary Biography* give biographical information on famous writers.

HOW CAN I GET IN TOUCH? DIRECTORIES

Q: Who is the director of the Society of Earthbound Extraterrestrials, and how can I contact him?

A: The director's name is Otomar Tllak and, although like E.T. he might advise you to "phone home," you can also contact him at the headquarters of the society at 408-486-3415. The address is 2140 Shattuck Avenue, Suite 2329, Berkeley CA 94704.

Source: *Encyclopedia of Associations.*[15]

Let's say you're doing a research paper on UFOs and you want to interview a real live person to add some pizzazz to your paper. Or maybe you just want to be sent some literature in the mail on a particular organization. To identify organizations, learn their missions, and find out how to get in touch with them, use the *Encyclopedia of Associations*, which may be available in electronic format at some libraries or in its traditional three-volume print format. This is not an encyclopedia in the true sense; it is more accurately defined as a directory, since it directs you to something.

The print version is arranged thematically, not alphabetically. The third volume, which provides an index to the first two, works a bit differently because it is a keyword index. The Society of Earthbound Extraterrestrials is listed three times in the alphabetically arranged index, once for each of the keywords in its title: **society**, **earthbound**, and **extraterrestrials**. Each time, the index refers you to 6713, which is the organization's entry number in the directory. Such a keyword index is very helpful when you can't remember an exact name or when you want to find out if there are groups that cover your interest. And once you locate the entry, you will notice that you are in the paranormal section of the directory, which includes other organizations such as the Amalgamated Flying Saucer Clubs of America, the Center for Bigfoot Studies, and the Ghost Research Society.

There are many other directories in the typical Reference Room, and an increasing number are available electronically. One book that we've already taken a look at, *Who's Who in America*, can be considered a directory as well as a source of biographical information because it provides contact information. Another important directory is the *United States Government Manual*, which tells you how to contact appropriate governmental agencies and officials. Any directory will tell you how to get in touch with real, live people, which are great sources of information.

SAY WHAT? QUOTATION BOOKS

Q: Who said the following:

1. "It's difficult to believe that people are starving in this country because food isn't available."
2. "I learned three important things in college —to use a library, to memorize quickly and visually, [and] to drop asleep at any time given a horizontal surface and fifteen minutes. What I could not learn was to think creatively on schedule."

A: 1. Ronald Reagan, the famous actor (in his most challenging role as President of the United States) during a press conference in 1986.
2. Agnes de Mille, the famous choreographer, in her book *Dance to the Piper*.

Sources: 1. *Bartlett's Familiar Quotations* [16]
2. *The New York Public Library Book of 20th Century American Quotations* [17]

Books of quotations serve three purposes:

1. to find quotes pertaining to a particular theme
2. to find some quotes attributed to a particular person
3. to find out who actually said a specific quote

There are two basic varieties of quotation books: thematically arranged and chronologically arranged. The best known book of quotations is *Bartlett's Familiar Quotations*, which belongs to the latter type, although you can also find quotes on specific themes by looking up keywords in the index (which actually takes up almost half of the volume). To answer the question above, you could look up the word "starving" in the index; there you would find: **Starving, difficult to believe people s., 730:16** which directs you to the Reagan quote above.

The source for the quotation from Agnes de Mille is a thematically arranged quotation book. Such compilations are great for finding a quote to use on a specific subject, but their focus on content means they tend to have much less detailed indexes in back, so it is often harder to use them to find the source of a quote you already know. The de Mille quote is in a chapter on education and college life.

WHERE DO I GO FROM HERE? BIBLIOGRAPHIES

Q: How many books were written about the Beatles between their rise to stardom in the early 1960s and their disbandment at the end of the decade?

A: Thirty, including such memorable works as *The Beatles: A Study in Drugs, Sex, and Revolution*, which contended that these four lads from Liverpool were really part of a communist plot to take over the world; and *Up the Beatles Family Tree*, a genealogical study of the band's members.

Source: *Popular Music: A Reference Guide.*[18]

Although you might think of a bibliography simply as the list of sources at the end of a book or as the list you must compile for your own research paper, there are also a wide variety of book-length bibliographies to be found in the typical Reference Room. These books can be enormously helpful, because they are focused on one particular subject and provide citations for books, periodical articles, audio-visual material, and rare unpublished works relating to the subject.

This concludes our little tour. I hope I've given you a general idea of what wonderful things can be found in the Reference Room as well as a few interesting facts you didn't already know. There's much more than I've mentioned here, obviously, and reference collections will differ from library to library. But no matter where you are, consider the Reference Room an oasis of information where your thirst for facts can be quenched.

NOTES

1. "Potato," *Academic American Encyclopedia*, 1995 ed.
2. "Czechoslovakia," *Encyclopedia Americana*, 1994 ed.
3. Jane and Michael Stern, *The Encyclopedia of Bad Taste* (New York: HarperCollins, 1990), 218.
4. Stuart Sutherland, *The International Dictionary of Psychology* (New York: Continuum, 1989), 325.
5. John Ayto and John Simpson, *The Oxford Dictionary of Modern Slang* (Oxford: Oxford University Press, 1992), 232.
6. Ira Konigsberg, *The Complete Film Dictionary* (New York: New American Library, 1987), 27.
7. "At Issue: Should Drugs be Legalized," in Mary H. Cooper, "War on Drugs," *The CQ Researcher*, 19 March 1993: 241–64.
8. *Editorials On File* (New York: Facts On File, 1994) 982–85.
9. *Statistical Abstract of the United States* (Washington, DC: U.S. Government Printing Office, 1994), 254.
10. *World Almanac and Book of Facts* (Mahwah, NJ: Funk and Wagnalls, 1995), 312, 742.

11. *Facts On File World News Digest* (New York: Facts On File, 1994), 236.
12. Bruce Wetterau, *New York Public Library Book of Chronologies* (New York: Prentice Hall, 1990), 552–57.
13. *Who's Who in America* (New Providence, NJ: Marquis, 1996), 1225.
14. *Current Biography Yearbook* (New York: H.W. Wilson, 1992), 511–14.
15. *Encyclopedia of Associations*, 29th ed. (Detroit: Gale Research, 1995), 1:858.
16. *The New York Public Library Book of 20th Century American Quotations* (New York: Warner Books, 1992), 165.
17. John Bartlett, *Familiar Quotations*, 16th ed. (Boston: Little, Brown, 1992), 730.
18. Roman Iwaschkin, *Popular Music: A Reference Guide* (New York: Garland, 1986), 226–32.

Five

Finding Your Way through Periodicals

I have helped numerous students who, before asking my advice, thought that the only way to find an article was to wander around the Periodical Room looking for an appropriately titled magazine or journal and then to browse through the issues. To offer an analogy I've used before, browsing for articles is like wandering through the desert looking for water. If you're lucky, you might find some, but you'll more likely die of thirst (or frustration) first.

This chapter will point you in the right direction, showing you the most efficient way to find articles using periodical indexes. These indexes, as I'll detail, are road maps for finding your way through periodicals, helping you to determine in exactly which issues you'll find articles on your topic.

JOURNALS VS. MAGAZINES

The first thing to understand about periodical indexes is the types of material they cover. Periodicals consist of anything published on a regular basis, be it daily, weekly, monthly, or quarterly. This includes newspapers, magazines, and journals. Despite the prevailing misconception, a journal is not the same thing as a magazine. *Journals* are periodicals containing articles written by experts in a particular field of study, frequently someone affiliated with an academic institution. They tend to be very specialized in their subject focus and are more *research oriented*. For example, let's say you picked up a copy of *People* magazine; you might see, as I did in some back issues, articles such as "The 50 Most Beautiful People in America" and "Brad Pitt, the Sexiest Man Alive." Were you to look at the table of contents of an issue of the *Journal of Popular Culture*, however, you'd see article titles like "Law as Soap Opera and Game Show: The Case of *The People's Court*," "Yes, Virginia, There is a Gender Difference: Analyzing Children's Requests to Santa Claus," or "Frankenstein as Founding Myth in Gary Larson's *The Far Side*." These articles sound like they might be just a bit more substantial than those in *People*, don't you think?

Journals contain a great deal of what is called *primary literature*. These are articles in which scholars who have conducted original research report their findings. *Secondary literature*, on the other hand, would be something like an article in *Time* magazine that discusses a recent development in nuclear physics—written by a reporter who had nothing to do with the actual research. His article would not go into as much technical depth because, aside from the fact that those who read a popular newsmagazine generally don't want all the scientific details, he is probably not an expert in the field of nuclear physics anyway, but instead a general science writer.

Journals even look different from magazines. While magazines tend to be glossy and colorful publications full of eye-catching graphics, journals are usually rather dull-looking and have dull-sounding titles that often, but not always, contain the word "journal." Despite this appearance, "don't judge a journal by its cover." Because journal articles are written by experts in a given field, the information they contain may prove more valuable for your own research than that which you would find in magazines. Sure, a magazine article is usually easier to read and understand, but, as a college student, you will need to use journals if you want to add any depth to your research. A bonus with journal articles is that they usually have extensive bibliographies that can lead you to further resources.

INDEXES: YOUR ROAD MAPS FOR FINDING ARTICLES

In chapter 4 I pointed out that the index in the back of a book is a very important tool. Instead of browsing through the entire book looking for what you need, you simply turn to the alphabetically arranged index in the back of the book and look up your subject to determine what page to turn to. Periodical indexes do the same sort of thing by referring you to articles in specific issues of various periodicals. Up until a few years ago, common periodical indexes were only available in book form. Each index covered periodicals in a different subject area, and a new volume of each usually became available every year.

But now, it seems that with each passing day more and more periodical indexes formerly available only in print are becoming available electronically. While many libraries subscribe to both the print and computerized versions, others have canceled their print subscriptions (although they keep the volumes they already have). New electronic periodical indexes that have no equivalent in book form have also become widely available.

Despite the prevalence of electronic indexes, I consider it important to understand how traditional print indexes are used for several reasons. In many libraries, they are still the only versions around of certain indexes; in fact, some indexes have no computerized equivalent because there is no electronic version on the market. Plus, computerized indexes tend to cover more recent periods of time, so if you want to find articles from the mid-1980s or before, you often have to use a print index. Sometimes, the computers at libraries are unavailable, either because it's the end of the semester and there are ten people in line ahead of you, or because of technical problems. In such cases, it's always good to be able to fall back on the old stand-bys on the shelf.

Whether you're using a computerized or print version of an index, the content remains the same; it's only the format that differs. So, if you understand what is contained in the print version of the *Readers' Guide*, or the *Social Sciences Index*, or the *General Science Index*, or any other index, you can approach a computerized index with confidence even if you've never used it before because the principles are the same; it's just the mode of searching that is different. By focusing on the content rather than the format of periodical indexes, this chapter will give you the background you need to more fully understand the electronic sources discussed in chapters 6 and 7. You will also obtain a more critical eye for selecting the appropriate index to serve your needs.

Readers' Guide—A "World Atlas" of Periodicals

Although *Readers' Guide* is now commonly found in its electronic form in many libraries and you may only have to use the print version to find articles before 1983, I want to go over how the print version works in some detail because it provides a clear example of how all other print indexes work.

The Readers' Guide to Periodical Literature, comprised of those thick green books that may look familiar to you from high school or your public library, is a general periodical index covering a wide variety of popular magazines like *Time, Newsweek,* and *People*. Volumes of *Readers' Guide* are published to cover the magazines of each year, going all the way back to 1900. When using *Readers' Guide*, or any print index that is composed of annual volumes, it is important to first consider which volume or volumes to consult.

As an example of how to use the *Readers' Guide*, let's say

you were writing a research paper on Woodstock—the first Woodstock music festival back in 1969, not the more recent festival of music (and mud) that occurred in 1994. Because of the date, you wouldn't be able to find articles using any electronic indexes because they usually don't go back more than a decade. So, if you go to the volume of *Readers' Guide to Periodical Literature* that covers the time period in which you're interested (it happens to be March 1969–February 1970) and look up **Woodstock,** you will see the entry in Figure 5.1, which tells you to see another heading and thus is a cross-reference. We previously discussed cross-references in relation to the online catalog in chapter 2; the principles are basically the same. The citations you want are actually categorized under **Music festivals—New York (state).** There is another type of cross-reference that begins with *see also*; this means that you will find citations under the heading you've looked up, but that you might also want to check out the other headings mentioned for related information. If you were to look up **Counterculture** in the 1993 volume of *Readers' Guide,* for example, it would tell you to *see also* **Beat generation, Cyberpunk, Punk culture, Rave culture,** and **Web jams.**

Getting back to our example, **Music festivals** is the main

WOODSTOCK college, Woodstock, Mass.
New American Jesuits. J. L'Heureux
   Atlan 224:59-64 N '69
WOODSTOCK music and art fair. See Music
   festivals - New York (state)
WOODSTONE, Norma Sue
   Help Wanted!! Mlle 6:130-1+ Je '69

Figure 5.1: *Readers' Guide to Periodical Literature*: **Woodstock** entry.

heading to look up; when you get there, find the subheading **New York (state)** (see Figure 5.2).

The first citation tells you about an article entitled "Age of Aquarius: Woodstock Music and Art Fair," which appeared in *Newsweek*. The **il**, standing for "illustrated," just means that the article has pictures. After the title of the magazine, you are provided with the volume number (74), which is just another way of referring to the year of publication; at the time this article appeared, *Newsweek* had been published for seventy-four years. Following the volume is the page number on which the article begins (88). Finally we are given the date of the issue that we need (August 25, 1969). Although the format of the citations might differ slightly, this is essentially the same information that you will see when using any index, whether print or electronic, because an index has to give you these essential facts to be of any use. Some indexes, primarily those that cover journals rather than magazines, also provide an issue number following the volume number.

Finding this information on Woodstock was not very dif-

MUSIC festivals - *Continued*

New York (state)
Age of Aquarius: Woodstock music and art
 fair. il Newsweek 74:88 Ag 25 '69
All nature is but art: Woodstock music and
 art fair. il Vogue 154:194-201 D '69
Big Woostock rock trip: with photographs by
 J. Dominis and B. Eppridge. Life 67: 14B-23
 Ag 29 '69

Figure 5.2: *Readers' Guide*: Entries under **Music festivals— New York (state)**.

ficult, but don't get too complacent. You will often be frustrated with print indexes because you may have a hard time determining the proper heading for your topic. This is similar to the problem I discussed in chapter 3 about the difficulties inherent in Library of Congress subject headings for books, and the same type of problem that will be encountered when trying to do subject rather than keyword searches in electronic indexes.

Suppose you have a more complex topic. You want to explore the ethical issues of cigarette and alcohol companies that target their advertising at specific ethnic groups, particularly African Americans. Which heading would you look under in *Readers' Guide*? You will discover, not surprisingly, that there is no such heading as **cigarette and alcohol advertising and African Americans**. Even if you broaden your search, you can't find **advertising and African Americans** or **cigarettes and African Americans**. After some experimenting, you decide to try the term **blacks** instead of **African Americans**. You then manage to find the headings **alcohol and blacks** and **smoking and blacks**, but many of these articles are not about advertising. You browse further and come upon a heading **cigarette industry/advertising** and **liquor industry/advertising**, but many of these articles are not about African Americans. When using a print index, you often need to skim through a list of citations under a more general heading. Computerized indexes offer a solution to this problem by providing the option of keyword searching, which I discussed in chapter 2.

Subject Indexes—The Local Road Maps to Periodicals

The *Readers' Guide* is like a world atlas of periodicals. In a world atlas, you only see general things such as country names and boundaries, major cities, oceans and seas, but you don't get a sense of the details of the landscape. You wouldn't use a world atlas if you were taking a road trip from Walla Walla, Washington, to Eureka, California. Instead, you'd want a more appropriate navigational tool like a detailed road atlas of the United States. In a more specific source such as this, you would be able to identify the major highways as well as secondary roads. You also might get a more detailed sense of the area's geographic features—lakes, rivers, mountains. Such specific road atlases are like the wide variety of subject indexes available in libraries for finding articles on more focused topics.

Just as you don't use a world atlas to plan a local trip, you don't use *Readers' Guide* to find articles on every topic. And you have to get beyond *Time, People*, and *Newsweek*, the tourist traps along the research roadway, when doing college-level research. Instead, look for subject-specific indexes to find articles in scholarly journals and other appropriate sources. The titles of these indexes will usually give you a clear indication of the types of periodicals they cover. I'll discuss a few of the more common ones in the next few pages to give you a sense of the logic you would use to select the appropriate index as well as to demonstrate some of the basic principles of searching an index. I have also provided a list of the most widely used indexes (Table 5.1), which may assist you in selecting the right one for your topic. But this list is by no means comprehensive; there are literally hundreds of indexes that are currently available, each one unique in the range of periodicals it covers.

Choosing and Using Subject Indexes: A Few Examples

Let's say you needed articles about Donald Trump's wheelings and dealings. You would probably be able to find some general articles in *Readers' Guide*, but you should also look in an index such as *Business Periodicals Index* which—as its title implies—focuses on business publications (the electronic equivalent is the CD-ROM *Wilson Business Abstracts*, which also provides summaries for all the articles cited) and covers magazines like *Business Week* and *Forbes* as well as trade journals. Trade journals, which are periodi-

Table 5.1 Selecting Which Index to Use:
A List of the Most Commonly Used Indexes

You Need	So Look at
General articles from popular magazines only	*Readers' Guide to Periodical Literature* *Readers' Guide Abstracts** *Magazine Index**
Articles on a wide range of subjects in magazines and/or journals	*General Periodical Index** *Academic Index ** *Expanded Academic Index** *Periodical Abstracts** *MasterFILE**
Articles from business magazines and trade journals	*Business Periodicals Index* *Wilson Business Abstracts** ABI/Inform*
Information about people	*Biography Index* *Biography Abstracts**
Book reviews	*Book Review Index* *Book Review Digest*
Literary criticism and journal articles on literary topics	*MLA International Bibliography*
Journal articles on a wide range of topics relating to the humanities including literature, performing arts, history, philosophy	*Humanities Index* *Humanities Abstracts**
Journal articles on a wide range of topics relating to social sciences including culture, geography, economics, politics	*Social Sciences Index* *Social Sciences Abstracts** *Sociological Abstracts*
Journal articles on topics relating to art	*Art Index* *Art Abstracts**
Articles in scientific journals and popular science magazines	*General Science Index* *General Science Abstracts**
Articles concerning the more technical aspects of science and their applications	*Applied Science and Technology Index* *Applied Science and Technology Abstracts**
Journal articles on psychology topics	*PsycLIT** and *PsycINFO** *Psychological Abstracts* print only

Table 5.1 (cont.)

Journal articles on education topics	*ERIC**
	RIE-Resources in Education print only
	CIJE-Current Index to Journals in Education print only
	Education Index
	Education Abstracts*
Articles from medical journals	*Medline**
	Index Medicus print only
Newspaper articles	*NewsBank* databases*
	Newspaper Abstracts *
	New York Times Index
	Other indexes provided by specific newspapers
Articles concerning political, economic, international and public affairs issues	*PAIS* (*Public Affairs Information Service*)
Government publications	*GPO Monthly Catalog*

Can't find what you need in any of the indexes listed above?
See a librarian for other suggestions.

* electronic only

---

cals written for people working in a specific industry, have intriguing titles such as *Beverage World* and *Progressive Grocer*. If you were to look in the August 1990–July 1991 volume of *Business Periodicals Index* or *Wilson Business Abstracts* under the heading **Trump, Donald J.**, you would find quite a number of article citations including "Donald Trump Just Won't Die" in *Fortune* magazine and "Opening the Taj: the Culture of Fantasy" in a trade journal called *The Cornell Hotel and Restauraunt Administration Quarterly*. The citation format looks exactly the same as that in *Readers' Guide* because the same company, H.W. Wilson, publishes both of them as well as a wide variety of other common indexes.

If you wanted more in-depth biographical information on "The Donald," you could look in *Biography Index*, which cites biographical material contained in a wider range of publications than is covered by *Readers' Guide*. Not only are there citations for magazine and journal articles on Ivana's "ex," but also books about him. While indexes are, for the most part, concerned with periodicals, there are some that cite books and book chapters. Figure 5.3 shows citations found under the heading **Trump, Donald J., real estate executive** in the print version of *Biography Index* (the same basic information will be found in the computerized format). You can tell that the first citation is for a book because there is no periodical title such as you see in the second citation. Instead there is only the name of the publisher (Simon & Schuster). Although the year of publication is cited in the book citation, there is not a more specific date included.

Let's move to a new topic and a different index. Suppose you were writing a paper on garbology—the study of garbage. You want to find out if the junk that people throw away can be used effectively to portray the society in which they live and if a garbage dump can be considered an archaeological site. How would you find articles on this?

One index you could check is the *Humanities Index,* which covers topics such as archaeology as well as history, literature, philosophy, religion, and the like. If you're using the print version, you'll have to determine which heading to look

```
O'Donnell, John R., and Rutherford, James. Trumped!;
   the inside story of the real Donald Trump - his
   cunning rise and spectacular fall. Simon &
   Schuster 1991 348p il
Plaskin, G. Ivana's heartache. il pors Ladies Home J
   107:76+ My '90
```

Figure 5.3: Sample entries from *Biography Index* under
Trump, Donald J.

under. As I have probably made clear by now, this is always the hardest part of using a print index. Looking up **garbology** is futile, because you won't find this heading in any volumes; there aren't even cross-references. You might try a keyword search in the electronic version, but still **garbology** might not bring up anything. When this happens, broaden your search and look under a more general term—for instance, simply **garbage**. Under this heading, you will find a cross-reference to **Refuse and refuse disposal**. And under that heading you'll find such intriguing article titles as "Monitoring Mississippian Homestead Occupation Span and Economy Using Ceramic Refuse" and "A Note on Some Scavengers of Ancient Egypt." You wouldn't find these treasures in *Readers' Guide* because they appear in scholarly journals.

Most of the more interesting topics that you'll research are interdisciplinary and cannot be narrowed down to one single area of study because they can be studied from various perspectives—scientific, sociological, literary, and so forth. Because of this, you can find articles on them in more than one index. When researching garbology, for instance, you could consult the *Social Sciences Index*, which covers periodicals that have a sociological emphasis. In this index, you would find an article entitled "Household Refuse Analysis: Theory, Method and Application in Social Science." There can be some overlap among indexes; some of the magazines or journals covered by one will be covered by another. But no two indexes cover the same exact set of periodicals.

Considering the interdisciplinary potential of this topic, you could also use the *General Science Index* for articles on the technical aspects of garbage analysis, or even *Art Index* for articles about garbage art. If you're unsure about which index to use, remember you can always ask a librarian.

Although I have limited my examples above to some of the popular Wilson indexes that have proven their usefulness over the years in their print format and are also now widely available electronically, they nonetheless demonstrate the basics of searching any print index. Be aware, however, that there are many other indexes besides these. So before we leave this section, let's look at abstracts and newspaper indexes.

Newspaper Indexes

Indexes for newspaper articles are special indexes. They're not focused on a specific topic; instead they cover stories on a wide variety of topics that have appeared in various newspapers. Some newspaper indexes, such as the *New York Times Index*, focus on just one paper. In fact, this was the norm until computerized indexes, such as *Newspaper Abstracts*, emerged with the capability to cover more than one newspaper; such indexes, however, generally only go back a few years, and often do not include every article that appeared in each paper.

Now suppose you had to do a report comparing the first Earth Day held back in 1970 with the twentieth-anniversary celebration in 1990. A good source would be newspaper articles, so you'd turn to a print index for the 1970 information since no computerized newspaper indexes go back that far. You could consult the *New York Times Index* as well as that for any other major newspaper that has its own index going back as far as 1970.

The old volumes of the *Times* index can be a bit unwieldy. If you look up **Earth Day** in the 1970 volume of the *New York Times Index*, you don't get a list of articles; instead you are provided with cross-references, the first one being **Air Pollution—NYC Met Area**. This is followed by dates: F1, Mr 19,27, Ap 17,20,21, Ap 23,24. You then look up the cross-referenced heading in the alphabetically arranged volume and find the actual citations arranged in date order and giving lengthy summaries. At the very end of the summary, also called an abstract, you will see the date, page number, and column number listed.

If you didn't have access to a good electronic newspaper index like *Newspaper Abstracts* and were to look up Earth

Day in the 1990 volume of the print *New York Times Index*, you'd probably notice, first of all, that it's better organized. There are also a couple of added features in the citations that you'll often see in both print and electronic formats. The length of the article is indicated by an (S), (M), or (L)—short, medium, or long—which can help you determine if the article is worth hunting down. In the *Times*, Roman numerals refer to the particular sections of the paper (other papers use letters to designate sections). Putting this all together, a medium-length article that appeared in the May 6th edition of the *Times* in section 2 on page 26 in the third column would be cited as follows: **(M), My 6, II, 26:3**.

Abstracts

There are a variety of indexes that have the word "abstracts" in their titles, like *Newspaper Abstracts*. These abstracts (in other words, "summaries") can be extremely helpful since it is often difficult to determine what an article is about from the title alone. Because these summaries take up a lot of space, it is becoming common for abstracts to be included in the electronic versions of indexes where space is not as big an issue as it is in print versions. Noncomputerized abstract indexes tend to be a bit unwieldy, and the computerized versions are much easier to deal with. But if you find yourself having to use the print version of an abstract index, ask a librarian for help if you encounter problems.

GENERAL RULES OF THE ROAD FOR GETTING THE ARTICLES

So once you know where to go, how do you actually get there? In other words, once you have citations, how do you get your hands on the articles? You'll definitely be asking yourself these questions if you've used a print index. And although more electronic indexes are providing the complete text of the articles they cite right on the screen, you will still often be asking yourself these same questions after using an electronic index. Since every library is arranged a bit differently, the paths will be somewhat varied, but I'll try to give you a general idea of how to arrive at your destination in the land of periodicals.

Hard Copy, Microfilm, and Electronic Formats

You will find articles in three basic formats: hard copy, microfilm, and electronic. While hard copies are the actual physical magazines, newspapers, or journals, microfilm provides a space-saving copy on film that can be read and reproduced by using a microfilm machine. Finally, there are an increasing number of computerized indexes that provide the complete text (and sometimes even graphics) of the articles they cite right on the screen.

At one time, microfilm was considered the latest in information technology, since a whole month's worth of newspapers or a year's worth of magazine issues could be fit on one tiny roll of film. Today, the computer revolution means the complete text of periodicals can be available online or on CD-ROM, and microfilm seems outdated, awkward, and simply a pain to use. Still, it is common in many libraries and will be around for some time to come. Just a technical note—occasionally you may need to use what is called *microfiche*; while the more prevalent microfilm is kept on rolls, microfiche comes in the form of cards. Together, both microfilm and microfiche are called *microforms*.

I have observed that many students, in an effort to avoid having to use microfilm, will only use hard-copy sources they can readily take off the shelf in the Periodical Room or, if they have discovered them, full-text electronic indexes. They will disregard any index citations that send them to go to the dreaded Microfilm Room. As a result, they may miss out on the most helpful information for their papers. My advice is not to judge a periodical source by its format but rather by its content. In the end, you'll be better off because having better sources makes it easier to write your research paper.

While magazines and newspapers are generally stored on microfilm, a year's issues of a scholarly journal are often bound into a single volume. Instead of each issue starting on page one, you'll notice that the volume is sequentially paginated like a book, with each issue comparable to a chapter.

Periodical Organization

Not all libraries organize their periodicals in the same way. In some libraries, periodicals (both hard copy and microfilm) are arranged alphabetically by title. In other libraries, each periodical may be assigned a call number depending on its subject focus. All the same rules of Library of Congress or Dewey Decimal call numbers (see chapter 3) then apply. Bound volumes of journals arranged by call number may be shelved in the Periodical Room or in the same stacks where circulating books are found. The best thing for you to do is just to become familiar with the way your library organizes its periodicals.

What If Your Library Doesn't Have It?

There are tens of thousands of magazines and journals being published in the world today, along with thousands of newspapers. With so many periodicals available, not every library can subscribe to every one, so academic libraries generally subscribe to what are known as the *core* (or most important) journals in those fields in which the college specializes. They may also get some of the *peripheral* (or less important) journals in these same fields as well as many general magazines as well as major newspapers like the *New York Times*, and the local papers for the area in which the library is located. Your library will either have a list of all its subscriptions or this information may be found in the online catalog, so you may be able to search for a periodical title in the same way you look for a book title.

If your library doesn't subscribe to the periodical you desperately need to complete your paper or have it available in electronic format through a full-text index, don't lose hope. If you have allotted yourself sufficient time for obstacles along the way (as I advised you to do in the beginning of this book), you can take advantage of the resources of other libraries.

A librarian can usually help you determine whether a periodical is in another library in your area. If the library is part of a consortium, there may be a list of the holdings of the other member libraries available. You can then either go to the library yourself to copy the article (since most periodicals do not leave the library) or you may even be able to have a copy sent to your own library.

If the periodical cannot be located in the immediate vicinity, your library can obtain it through Interlibrary Loan. If the article you need is in an obscure scholarly journal held by only a handful of libraries in the country, your library's ILL department can request this article and usually get it to you within a week or two. The time factor involved here is the main drawback of ILL and the reason that many students, starting their papers too late, cannot take advantage of this valuable service.

Another option is to get articles through commercial document delivery services. One such service is called UnCover, through which, for a fee, you can have any article in over 17,000 periodicals faxed to you within twenty-four hours. FirstSearch, which will be described in the next chapter, also provides a document delivery service. So if you're desperate to get something quickly, ask your librarian if these or other services are available at your library.

TAKING THE "ROAD LESS TRAVELED" THROUGH THE PERIODICAL ROOM

When I was out in Arizona a few years ago visiting a college friend in Tucson, the lure of the open road inspired us on a particularly beautiful afternoon to take a road trip up to historic Route 66, the first "highway" constructed between Chicago and California back in the 1920s. During the Depression and up until the construction of the parallel Interstate–40 in the 1970s, this two-lane road was the major east-west route. Since then, however, long stretches of Route 66 have either crumbled into disrepair or been paved over by the speedier superhighway. But other sections have been maintained, and tourists are beginning to rediscover the value of this road as they "get their kicks on Route 66." With all its roadside pit stops, hamburger joints, neon signs, teepees, ghost towns, and other campy attractions, it has become a living museum of American culture and history, while the interstate highway that runs nearby is about as interesting as reading the phonebook. Even though Route 66 is a "road less traveled" by people who want to get to their final destination quickly, it certainly provides those who do take the time to explore it with a more unique experience.

Although electronic indexes are a virtual interstate superhighway through the Periodical Room, don't forget that you may still on occasion benefit from using a print index. The same holds true for making the effort to use microfilm instead of limiting yourself to the more recent and accessible periodicals. Like driving along Route 66 instead of taking I–40, you may find some unusual things. Remember what Robert Frost wrote: "Two roads diverged in a wood, and I— I took the one less traveled by, and that has made all the difference." Although electronic resources are more frequently used these days, a print resource may still provide you with the information that will make "all the difference" in your paper.

Six

Different Modes of Electronic Transportation

Sometimes you drive a car to your destination. At other times you might need to use a truck or ride the bus. For instance, some students rent trucks to bring all their essential belongings to college because they can't possibly stuff everything they'll need for comfortable dorm living into their parents' car. And despite my own love for the freedom of the open road and my extended use of the road trip metaphor to describe the research process, I currently use public transportation because of the city where I live.

As I'll discuss later in this chapter, riding a bus or a truck is like using an online database, while driving your own car is like using a CD-ROM database. Remember that a database is any collection of information stored in an electronic form, be it an index providing citations to other material or a full-text source actually providing the entire work. Before discussing the differences between online and CD-ROM databases and pointing out some of the more popular sources you are likely to encounter, however, let's get some background information.

WHAT IS A CD-ROM?

You were probably first introduced to compact discs as a musical medium that has revolutionized the music industry. Because of its superior sound quality and the convenient access it provides to the songs encoded on it, the CD has caused vinyl records to become virtually obsolete. The same technology that is used to create music CDs, however, can also be used to produce discs, called CD-ROMs, that store data in many forms—text, graphics, animation, and video, as well as sound. CD-ROMs have revolutionized information technology, and a CD-ROM drive, which is needed to read the data and make it accessible through a computer, is now standard equipment in libraries.

CD-ROM stands for *compact disc—read only memory*, meaning that once data is encoded on the disc, it can't be altered, only read. One revolutionary aspect of the CD-ROM is its capacity to hold information, a capacity that seems to be ever increasing as the technology continues to develop; a CD-ROM currently can hold the equivalent of about 325,000 pages of text—quite an improvement over the 500 pages that a traditional 3-1/2" floppy disc can hold. This huge capacity has extraordinary implications for libraries. An entire encyclopedia, for instance, can fit on one disc; so can a periodical index that takes up a whole shelf in its print format.

The other revolutionary aspect of CD-ROMs is how the user can instantaneously access any piece of information contained on the disc. CD-ROMs, as computerized databases, are searchable in much the same way as an online book catalog. So despite the tremendous amount of material contained on a CD-ROM, you can easily find what you need. (In chapter 7, I will build upon the fundamentals already covered about Boolean searching and show you how to effectively focus in on your topic whether you are searching a CD-ROM or an online database.)

The manner in which you access CD-ROMs will differ from library to library. In some libraries, the entire collection of CD-ROMs may be loaded in a "jukebox" that holds multiple discs so that all you have to do is select the appropriate one from a menu screen. At other libraries, however, there may only be a disc drive that holds a single disc so you'll need to request the CD-ROM you want at the Reference Desk. The CD-ROM collection may be accessible from several computers at the same time so that more than one person can use a database simultaneously, or a disc may only be accessible by one user at a time. There may be computer workstations devoted to using CD-ROMs, or you may be able to select them from a menu on the same terminal where you use the online catalog. Because of all these variations, the best tactic is simply to become familiar with the logistics at your particular library.

WHAT IS AN ONLINE DATABASE?

You'll recall from chapter 2, in which online public access catalogs (OPACs) were discussed, that online simply refers to the connection between computers. When one computer is properly connected to another computer, the two of them can exchange information. So an online database is simply a collection of information that you access by connecting to the computer storing the database, which is the server. Although a computerized library catalog is an online database, the types of online resources I will be discussing in this chapter are periodical indexes and full-text sources rather than databases containing records for items in a particular institution. A library subscribes to these online databases or pays a fee one lump sum to subscribe to a database or pays a small fee for each search performed in it.

These days, online access is coming to mean access through the World Wide Web. When an online database is available on the Web, it does not mean that it is free and anyone can get into it. Although a lot of free information is on the World Wide Web, an increasing proportion of Web resources have restricted access. It is the cost and quality of commercial online databases that differentiate them from the free Internet and World Wide Web sources I will discuss in chapter 8; but fundamentally, the Web is really just one huge and messy online database.

You may already be familiar with online services like CompuServe and America Online, which, among other things, provide full-text coverage of various publications. Since these are commercial services intended for individuals to use at home on their personal computers rather than at libraries, they don't really fit into the scope of this book.

You should be aware that many CD-ROM databases also have online versions. For instance, *Readers' Guide Abstracts*, the computerized version of the *Readers' Guide to Periodical Literature*, is available both on CD-ROM and online. SilverPlatter, a prolific producer of CD-ROMs, is also providing access to a growing number of its titles online.

DIFFERENCES BETWEEN CD-ROM AND ONLINE RESOURCES

Personal Vehicles vs. Public Transportation

A CD-ROM database, which can often cost thousands of dollars, is purchased by the library and costs the same whether 1,000 searches are done per month or 100 or 10. CD-ROMs are therefore most cost-effective for databases that get used often, like *Readers' Guide Abstracts*. Although I know you couldn't care less about these financial implications for libraries, stick with me for just a little bit and you'll understand why you'll be going online to access some databases but using CD-ROMs to access others.

Some indexes are not used frequently enough by a library to justify buying a CD-ROM version, because the cost per search would be too high. In that case, there is an online alternative. Some online databases incur a cost only for the time they are used or for the number of searches performed in them, just as you would pay per ride when taking the bus. This cost is usually paid by the library rather than by you, the student. The bottom line that should interest you is that databases that your library could otherwise not afford to provide can be made available for your research. Online databases may be available through your library's online catalog terminals or at separate workstations.

One of the advantages of CD-ROMs, however, is that they can work more quickly. You will often find that online databases can have a slow response time. This is because of high use on the network over which you access them. It's sort of like the difference between hopping in your own car and having to wait for the bus.

Carrying the Load

As I mentioned before, online databases can also be compared to renting a truck. Despite the huge storage capacity of CD-ROMs, sometimes databases get so large that even a CD-ROM that can hold the equivalent of about 325,000 pages of text cannot contain the database. For example, there are databases that provide the complete text for several years' worth of all the major daily newspapers in the United States. No single CD-ROM would be able to hold such a tremendous amount of data. Just as you need to rent a truck if your car is too small to carry your load, you need to have a bigger storage place if your information load is too big for a CD-ROM. So you go online when you need to access a database too large to fit on a CD-ROM because this enables you to connect with a server having enormous storage capacity. This computer could be across town or in another state. As long as you're hooked up properly, it really doesn't matter.

Driving the Latest Model

A final, important difference between CD-ROM and online databases is that online sources can provide more current information. Because these databases are stored in a central location, they can easily be updated weekly or even daily; CD-ROMs are usually only updated on a monthly or quarterly basis, because each time they are changed new discs have to be mailed out to all the subscribers. Some online databases can give you citations for articles in last week's newspapers and magazines rather than last month's. This can be extremely valuable for many current topics.

ADVANTAGES OF ELECTRONIC DATABASES

Both CD-ROM and online versions of print sources share many advantages over print. First of all, due to the huge storage capacity of CD-ROMs and the almost limitless capacity of online resources, multiple volumes of an index can be stored in a single database. For example, it is possible to fit ten volumes (ten whole years!) of the print *Readers' Guide to Periodical Literature* on just one CD-ROM; instead of having to look up your subject ten times in ten different annual volumes, you just type it in once to get a list of articles in descending chronological order for the past ten years. The computerized *Readers' Guide* also contains summaries of the articles, which is why its official title is *Readers' Guide Abstracts*; a full-text version has also recently become available. Although abstracts are provided in some print indexes, as we've noted, this is not usually practical because they take up too much space. Due to the tremendous capacity of computerized resources, however, abstracts and even complete text are often included. Another benefit is you can either print out the citations and/or text that you want or download the information to your own floppy disc, rather than having to copy the information down by hand or find the hard copy of the article.

The greatest advantage of using computerized indexes is the ease with which they can be searched. (We will walk through this process in the next chapter.) The problem with print indexes—the same one that you may have when looking for books under subject headings in the online catalog— is that you may often have difficulty finding the appropriate subject heading for your topic—say your topic is too complex to be defined by a single heading. You can, however, search computerized databases by keyword.

TYPES OF DATABASES

The most common electronic databases found in libraries today are computerized indexes. Indexes, as you'll recall from the previous chapter, give you citations that indicate in which periodicals you can find articles on a certain topic; electronic indexes are also called *bibliographic databases*. Bibliographic citations may even include brief abstracts of the articles. But you may also encounter CD-ROM and online indexes that provide the actual text of articles right on the screen, eliminating the need to hunt them down elsewhere in the library. These are *full-text databases* as opposed to bibliographic databases. There are also *full-image databases*, which display exact reproductions of articles, including both text and graphics.

Many encyclopedias, directories, and other traditional reference sources are becoming available on CD-ROM and online. Having read chapter 4, you are already familiar with books like *Encyclopedia of Associations*, *Current Biography*, and *Facts On File World News Digest*. These and many other titles can now be used electronically, providing the same information as the original sources, but in an easier-to-search format. Instead of flipping through the index in the back of a book searching for an appropriate heading, just enter keywords on a search screen and instantly find what you need.

Many reference sources on CD-ROM and an increasing number of online sources—especially those accessible through the World Wide Web—employ multimedia technology, which combines text with graphics, animation, video, and/or sound. This provides a new and exciting way to present reference material. For instance, *Grolier's Multimedia Encyclopedia* contains on a single disc not only the twenty-one volumes of the *Academic American Encyclopedia* but also additional pictures, maps, animation, video, sound, and more. You can look up John Kennedy and, in addition to reading about him, actually watch a video of him giving a number of important speeches. As you read the text, you might see a term highlighted like Vietnam. If you click on this term, you immediately jump to the article that describes this topic in more detail. The ability to jump between related topics like this is referred to as *hypertext* (we'll get to it in chapter 8, when we hop on the Internet). Basically it means that there is no inherent structure such as a traditional encyclopedia arranged in alphabetical order would have. As a result, the path you chose to take is determined by your curiosity.

SELECTING ELECTRONIC INDEXES

Just as with print indexes, there are many different electronic indexes, and it is vital to select the appropriate one. For example, although the *Readers' Guide Abstracts* might provide citations for a number of articles on a subject like beer microbreweries, you would probably find additional material using the electronic *Wilson Business Abstracts*.

When selecting an electronic index, the same rules apply as when choosing a print one. Table 5.1 provides a succinct list to help you answer the question, "What index do I use?" Of course, not every library will have every one of these sources and some libraries will certainly have sources not mentioned in this table; some libraries might still have the print version, while others will have access to the electronic version. If you get confused by the variety of indexes available to you, just think of how mind-boggling it can sometimes be to buy a new car, decide what size truck you should rent, or figure out the best bus route. Remember that reference librarians are available to assist you in selecting the appropriate resources and they're usually more helpful than car dealers.

POPULAR CD-ROM PRODUCERS AND ONLINE SERVICES

For the remainder of this chapter, I will describe in greater detail the CD-ROM and online databases you will be most likely to encounter in a typical college library. Although there are many others, these examples will demonstrate the principles common to all. Currently, two of the most popular online services designed for library users are FirstSearch and InfoTrac, so I will look at these two to demonstrate the exciting potential of online resources.

First Search

FirstSearch, produced by an organization called OCLC, is a collection of databases. FirstSearch gives library users access to over sixty databases, including many of the indexes we've already mentioned—with the additional feature of abstracts. You will find *Readers' Guide Abstracts, Humanities Abstracts*, and *General Science Abstracts* here, as well as many other more specialized indexes. A few of the databases, however, are full-text reference sources like *Disclosure*, which contains financial reports for companies nationwide, and the *Concise Columbia Electronic Encyclopedia*.

The screens displayed in Figures 6.1 and 6.2 are taken

from the new World Wide Web version of FirstSearch. If your library has FirstSearch but is using the older version, the screen will not look as pretty but the content will be the same. Also, some libraries choose to block certain databases if they already subscribe on CD-ROM.

Figure 6.1 shows the Database Area selection screen, which is where you begin your searching:

You can choose "All Areas" if you are unsure of which specific area to select; this will display a listing of all the databases, or you can try something more specific. If you wanted to find newspaper articles on a subject, for instance, select "News & Current Events," which will bring up the list of databases shown in Figure 6.2. These are the ones out of the almost sixty available that pertain to news and current events. From this list you can choose *NewsAbs*, the First-Search version of *Newspaper Abstracts*, an index to over twenty-five major metropolitan newspapers. After an initial introductory screen, the main search screen will be displayed. (We'll look at a specific search in *NewsAbs* in chapter 7.)

As an online service, FirstSearch has some advantages over CD-ROMs. A recently added feature is the option of

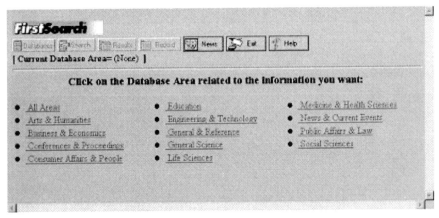

Figure 6.1: FirstSearch's Database Area selection screen.

viewing the complete text for some of the articles cited in a few of the index databases, or even having them e-mailed or faxed to you. These new options incur an added cost, however, so if your library does have FirstSearch, it may not allow you to use them. An additional benefit is that many of the databases accessed through FirstSearch are updated more frequently than are their CD-ROM or print equivalents. *Newspaper Abstracts*, for example, is updated weekly. FirstSearch really opens up the road before you, allowing a library to provide computerized versions of a much larger number of databases than it would ever be able to afford in CD-ROM versions. In fact, some FirstSearch databases don't even have CD-ROM equivalents, so this online service offers their only electronic access.

InfoTrac

Information Access Company produces InfoTrac databases that not only give you citations for articles but also often provide the complete text of these articles right on the screen, along with their graphics. Although my example is taken from the older version, which does not display images,

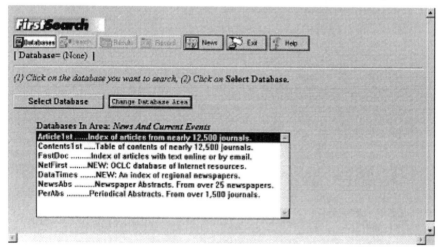

Figure 6.2: FirstSearch's Database selection screen.

the new World Wide Web–accessible InfoTrac SearchBank does. So let me show you what a full-text database looks like.

One of InfoTrac's databases is *Expanded Academic Index*, which indexes 1,500 periodicals (both popular magazines and scholarly journals) in a variety of subject categories. A version of this index, called *Expanded Academic ASAP*, provides the added feature of full-text for about one-third of the periodicals covered by *Expanded Academic Index*. *Expanded Academic Index* and *ASAP* are best used for topics of a more current nature, since they only cover the past four years (unless your library subscribes to the back files).

Suppose you needed recent articles about the legalization of marijuana. If you do a keyword search in *Expanded Academic ASAP* for **marijuana and legalization**, you will get the list of records shown in Figure 6.3. At the end of each citation, you are told if an abstract and/or the text of the article are available. After selecting citation number 2, for example, which provides the complete text, you would first see the expanded citation and abstract, as in Figure 6.4. On the

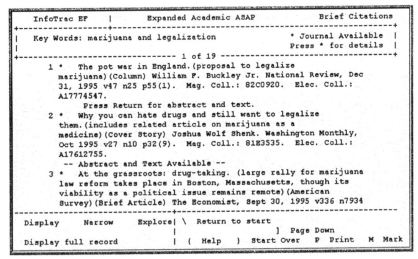

```
    InfoTrac EF      |      Expanded Academic ASAP         Brief Citations
+--------------------+----------------------------------------------------+
|  Key Words: marijuana and legalization              * Journal Available  |
|                                                     Press * for details  |
+------------------------------ 1 of 19 ------------------------------------+
     1 *   The pot war in England.(proposal to legalize
           marijuana)(Column) William F. Buckley Jr. National Review, Dec
           31, 1995 v47 n25 p55(1).  Mag. Coll.: 82C0920.  Elec. Coll.:
           A17774547.
           Press Return for abstract and text.
     2 *   Why you can hate drugs and still want to legalize
           them.(includes related article on marijuana as a
           medicine)(Cover Story) Joshua Wolf Shenk. Washington Monthly,
           Oct 1995 v27 n10 p32(9).  Mag. Coll.: 81E3535.  Elec. Coll.:
           A17612755.
           -- Abstract and Text Available --
     3 *   At the grassroots: drug-taking. (large rally for marijuana
           law reform takes place in Boston, Massachusetts, though its
           viability as a political issue remains remote)(American
           Survey)(Brief Article) The Economist, Sept 30, 1995 v336 n7934
-------------------------------+------------------------------------------
  Display      Narrow     Explore| \  Return to start
                                 |                  ]  Page Down
  Display full record            |  ( Help  )  Start Over   P  Print   M  Mark
```

Figure 6.3: Records retrieved through a keyword search for **marijuana and legalization** in *Expanded Academic ASAP*.

following screen, as displayed in Figure 6.5, the actual text of the article appears. Although this nongraphical version hardly looks like what you'd see if you opened the actual magazine, the content is basically the same.

When you use *Expanded Academic ASAP* or any similar database that provides complete text for selected articles, don't overlook the records that don't offer complete texts just because you can't obtain them so easily. When you're doing research, you shouldn't choose your information based on how easy it is to get your hands on it. Instead, try taking "the road less traveled" and see where it leads. Your library might actually subscribe to the periodicals that are not available in full-text electronic format. Remember that the primary function of *Expanded Academic ASAP* and other databases like it is to be an index, not a one-stop shopping center.

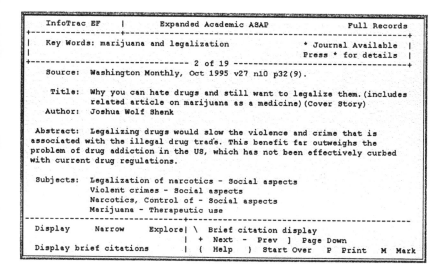

Figure 6.4: Record for an article on the legalization of marijuana in *Expanded Academic ASAP*.

Wilson Indexes

In addition to being available in traditional print format, the ever popular Wilson indexes such as *Readers' Guide* and numerous others are available on CD-ROM as well as online through FirstSearch, Wilson's own WILSONLINE, and other online services. Most of these electronic versions now provide abstracts for the articles cited. So a database such as *Humanities Abstracts*, for example, is really just *Humanities Index* with the added feature of article summaries. A full-text version of *Readers' Guide* is also now available.

SilverPlatter

SilverPlatter is another popular provider of CD-ROMs and online databases. Unlike Wilson, they do not actually produce the content of these databases but are responsible for developing the software that makes the databases work. The important thing to note is that if you hear someone refer to SilverPlatter, they are not referring to a specific database but

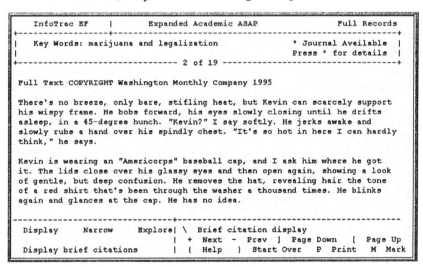

```
   InfoTrac EF    |      Expanded Academic ASAP              Full Records
+------------------+------------------------------------------------------------+
|   Key Words: marijuana and legalization              * Journal Available   |
|                                                      Press * for details   |
+----------------------------- 2 of 19 ------------------------------------+

Full Text COPYRIGHT Washington Monthly Company 1995

There's no breeze, only bare, stifling heat, but Kevin can scarcely support
his wispy frame. He bobs forward, his eyes slowly closing until he drifts
asleep, in a 45-degree hunch. "Kevin?" I say softly. He jerks awake and
slowly rubs a hand over his spindly chest. "It's so hot in here I can hardly
think," he says.

Kevin is wearing an "Americorps" baseball cap, and I ask him where he got
it. The lids close over his glassy eyes and then open again, showing a look
of gentle, but deep confusion. He removes the hat, revealing hair the tone
of a red shirt that's been through the washer a thousand times. He blinks
again and glances at the cap. He has no idea.

------------------------------------------+-----------------------------------
  Display     Narrow     Explore| \  Brief citation display
                              |  + Next  - Prev  ] Page Down  [ Page Up
  Display brief citations      |  { Help  } Start Over  P Print  M Mark
```

Figure 6.5: Full-text article displayed in *Expanded Academic ASAP*.

to the company that produces the databases. I mention this because students sometimes come to me asking for SilverPlatter. I then ask them if they want *ERIC*, *Medline*, or *PsycLIT*, three of the common indexes available through SilverPlatter. You might have the same misunderstanding about FirstSearch and InfoTrac; remember that these are collections of databases, not indivdual ones. Think of it this way: if you go to a Toyota dealer, you probably won't ask to see a Toyota; instead you'll certainly want to pick a specific model (a Corolla, a Tercel, a Camry) that will serve your needs.

ProQuest

ProQuest CD-ROM databases are produced by a company called UMI, which has been at the forefront of providing full-text databases including *Periodical Abstracts PlusText* and full-image databases such as *General Periodicals Index*. They also produce a number of index and abstract CD-ROM databases such as *Newspaper Abstracts* (which they make accessible online through FirstSearch) and *ABI/INFORM,* a good source of business information. Through UMI InfoStore, a document delivery service, you can obtain the articles for which the complete text is not already available as part of the database.

LEXIS/NEXIS

Although usually only found in larger research universities, I just want to briefly mention LEXIS/NEXIS because, even in the small library where I work, I am frequently asked if we have it. Provided by Reed-Elsevier, LEXIS/NEXIS is best known for its depth of full-text coverage and current information. It is composed of two distinct parts: LEXIS, a full-text legal information service that has been available since 1973, and NEXIS, a full-text news and business information service introduced in 1979 providing access to electronic versions of newspapers and magazines, world news services, newswire services, and television transcripts. Many of these sources are updated daily. With the proliferation of other cheaper and easier-to-use full-text online services, however, the need for LEXIS/NEXIS is diminishing in general libraries, although corporate and legal libraries still depend upon it.

DIALOG

As you'll understand after reading this description, DIALOG is the end of the road. The DIALOG online service, which is provided by Knight-Ridder Information, has been available since 1972. It currently consists of over 450 online databases that together cover just about any subject you could think of, from accounting to zoology. These 450 databases contain over 330 million abstracts, citations, and full-text articles. Some of the databases are very specific, such as *AIDSLINE*, which is an index solely to literature about AIDS. DIALOG is well known for its variety of excellent business and technical resources and is an essential tool in most corporate libraries. Using these resources you would be able to find, among many other things: financial information on over 12 million American companies, descriptions of 10 million chemical substances, and data on over 15 million patents. The amount of information available through DIALOG is staggering. Although many of the databases available are indexes and directories, a large number provide complete text, including the *PAPERS* database, which covers all major newspapers in the United States. So why isn't everyone lining up to use this astounding online library?

Fundamentally, cost prohibits academic libraries from letting students have unlimited access to DIALOG. Each of the 450 databases charges a different rate, and some of the more specialized business databases cost hundreds of dollars per hour. And because extensive training is required to use this service cost effectively, librarians perform searches rather than students. If your library offers DIALOG searching, as many academic libraries do, it will only be used after all other available resources in the library have been exhausted. Obviously, if the information you need can be obtained from a CD-ROM, that will be used first.

Fortunately, for the purposes of this book, I don't need to explain to you how to use DIALOG since most likely you will never have to use it yourself unless you decide to enter the "information retrieval business" (also known by the less glamorous term of "librarianship"). You should just be aware that a huge array of databases exists aside from the ones that are available for the public to use in your library. When you encounter a roadblock in your research, ask a librarian if the DIALOG service is available, and, if so, might there be an appropriate DIALOG database that could provide you with the information that you need. Just knowing that this service exists and is available for the asking in most academic libraries puts you miles ahead of the average student.

There are certainly other CD-ROM producers and online service providers that I have not covered here. But this book is not intended to turn you into a librarian. Being familiar with the major databases you are likely to encounter is sufficient and can help you to understand the other lesser known ones that also may be available in your library. Just as there are many different modes of transportation (cars, trucks, buses, trains, motorcycles, RVs—and all their variations), there are different resources for different research topics. Each serves a purpose, and each must be chosen with your need in mind.

Seven

Focusing Your Explorations

W hat would a road trip be without taking a few pictures—snapshots of you and your traveling buddies enjoying the freedom of the highway, the majestic scenery passing by your window, and the road itself stretching out in front of you to the distant horizon. To capture these moments on film, you need to look through the viewfinder and decide what you want to include in your photograph, and then bring it into focus.

When you do research, you'll treasure in a different way the material that helps you complete your project. You probably won't keep your articles in a scrapbook or album and look back upon them fondly years later (unless you're really obsessed with your topic). But they'll certainly be of great value as you look back upon them and write your research paper. But in order to find such valuable material, you have to know how to focus on your topic when using an electronic database just as you focus on an object when taking a picture. This chapter will show you how to do this.

Although the sources I will be discussing in the following pages may not be the ones that you will be using in your library, they clearly demonstrate the basic principles of how to search any computerized database. In fact, you will recognize some of these techniques from chapter 2's discussion of searching online catalogs—techniques that will even be used in searching the World Wide Web. I don't want to get bogged down in specifics here since, considering the rapidity of change, that would be quite futile. What's important, as always, is the underlying theory. As I've said before, just as the controls of a car may differ slightly but not affect the basic way you drive, so these databases may differ from others but still employ the same basic searching rules.

BASIC SEARCHING TECHNIQUES

One quick reminder: since the following databases are constantly being updated, the results I have retrieved here in these examples will be different from what would be retrieved at a later time. The numbers of records retrieved are only given as examples.

A Basic Subject Search Using *Readers' Guide Abstracts*

Readers' Guide Abstracts is the electronic version of the *Readers' Guide to Periodical Literature* and is available in both CD-ROM and online format. Figure 7.1 demonstrates the initial screen for the *Readers' Guide Abstracts* CD-ROM (version 3.0). The first option on this menu screen, "Single subject search," enables you to look up a single term and is effective for simple topics. It's like looking up a book by a Library of Congress subject heading. A "Multiple subject search" is used for more complex topics, allowing you to enter multiple terms to accurately define your topic. This type of search offers the same flexibility that keyword searching provides to an online catalog. Most searchable electronic databases offer both a simple and more complex mode of searching. A "Command language disc search" is an even more advanced form of keyword searching that you probably won't need to use in this database, so I'll skip it for the purposes of this discussion.

Suppose you were interested in researching the cultural phenomenon of "couch potatoes." Choose the single subject

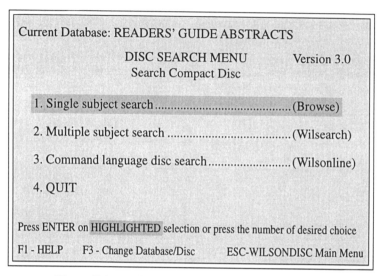

Figure 7.1: *Readers' Guide Abstracts* opening menu.

search option from the opening menu and enter **couch potatoes** in the search box, as displayed in Figure 7.2. After entering the heading, the portion of the alphabetical subject heading list containing your specified search term will appear, as in Figure 7.3. The numbers to the left of each subject heading tell you how many article citations have been found on the topic. The asterisks to the left of headings mean that a *different term* should be used; in this version of the database you simply follow the directions at the top of the screen and press the key specified (in this case F8) in order to find out what term to use. Many indexes have such a system of cross-referencing. But if you enter a heading that doesn't appear at all in the list, not even with a cross-reference, try another search using a synonym.

In this particular edition of *Readers' Guide*, nineteen articles have been located under the general heading **couch potatoes**. Beneath the main heading, more specific subject headings such as **couch potatoes/health and hygiene** are listed from which you can choose if you want to narrow this topic.

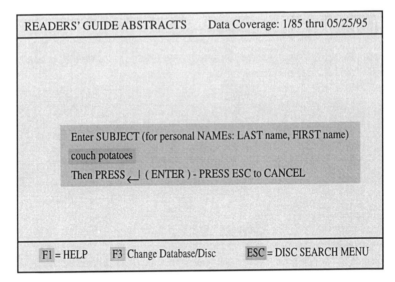

Figure 7.2: Single subject search for **couch potatoes**
in *Readers' Guide*.

READERS' GUIDE ABSTRACTS   Data Coverage: 1/85 thru 05/25/95

Press ENTER to see entries for HIGHLIGHTED subject - F8 to see related subjects
05/25/95

ENTRIES	SUBJECT
1	COTUGNO, GIANLUCA
*	COTUNRISM
*	COTURNIX
*	COTY AWARDS
1	COTYLEDONS (GUY) (FIRM)
19	COUCH POTATOES
1	COUCH POTATOES/ANECDOTES, FACETIAE, SATIRE, ETC.
8	COUCH POTATOES/HEALTH AND HYGIENE
3	COUCH POTATOES/NUTRITION
5	COUCH TRIP (MOTION PICTURE REVIEW)
1	COUCH TRIP (VIDEO TAPE REVIEW)
1	COUCH, CHRIS

>>>>>> Begin typing to BROWSE a new SUBJECT <<<<<<

| F1 = HELP   ESC = MENU | ↑ = Move UP | PgUp = Previous | 12 subjects |
| F3 Change Database/Disc | ↓ = Move DOWN | PgDn = Next | 12 subjects |

Figure 7.3: Subject list indicating number of article citations
found in *Readers' Guide*.

Figure 7.4 shows a sample record found under the heading **couch potatoes**. This record contains all of the same information that could be found in the print version: the author and title of the article and the periodical, or source, in which the article can be found. These are fundamental components of any citation. In addition, you get an abstract of the article.

A FirstSearch Search

For another example of basic searching techniques, I want to return to a database we encountered in the last chapter, *NewsAbs* available through FirstSearch. To actually perform a search you need to be at the main search screen, as seen in Figure 7.5.

As you will notice, the fundamental ways to search this database as well as most of the other FirstSearch databases are by subject, author, and title. Subject searching, which is used most often, is actually more like keyword searching

---

READERS' GUIDE ABSTRACTS   Data Coverage: 1/85 thru 05/25/95

Line   1 of   21 lines

SUBJECT is COUCH POTATOES   1 of 19 Entries
#1

    AUTHOR: Livingston, Kathryn E.
      TITLE: Is your child a couch potato?
    SOURCE: Redbook (ISSN: 0034-2106) v 101 p 176-7 September '93
  CONTAINS: illustration (s)

SUBJECTS COVERED:
Children/Physical Fitness
Couch potatoes

ABSTRACT: Part of a special section on coping with children's school problems. According to the National Children and Youth Fitness Study II of 1987, 36 percent of elementary-school children take physical education (PE) classes daily, but only 37 percent have PE only once or twice a week. The study also found that kids spend only 2 or 3 minutes in vigorous activity in an average class. Experts say that inadequate gym classes.

    ENTER ↵ for Next Entry/ESC to STOP DISPLAY   PgDn/END/↓ to Scroll Down

ESC   = STOP Displaying Entries - Resume BROWSING Subjects   F1 = HELP
F2   = BROWSE a NEW Subject   F4 = PRINT this Entry   F5 = Go to an Entry
F6   = PRINT all Entries from HERE to the print limit

Figure 7.4: A typical *Readers' Guide* record.

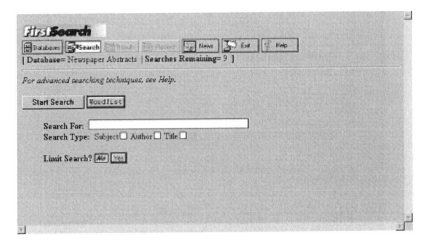

Figure 7.5: Basic search screen for a FirstSearch database.

because, in addition to searching the subject headings, the title, abstract, and notes fields are also searched. There are more advanced searching techniques that allow you to determine the best subject headings by browsing through something called the wordlist; you can also perform additional searches on a person's name or a specific newspaper and use the limit command to narrow down your search to a certain year or a particular kind of material. In this database, for example, you could limit your search to certain categories such as newspaper interviews, book reviews, or feature articles. If your library has FirstSearch, you can learn these advanced techniques by clicking on the "Help" button, but for the sake of illustration and to avoid making this chapter too long and overwhelming, I'll be sticking to the basics here.

To return to our example, enter **prozac** and select "subject" as the search type. Figure 7.6 shows part of the list of records retrieved. You might wonder what "Snow White on Prozac" is all about, but if you were to read the abstract included in the full record, you would realize that the article has actually nothing to do with Prozac. Why was it re-

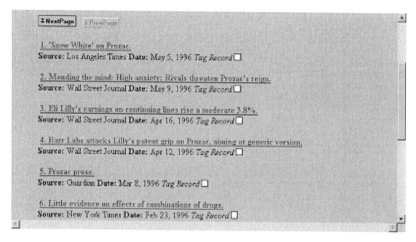

Figure 7.6: A FirstSearch list of records.

trieved? Remember, in performing this search the term **prozac** was located in subject headings as well as titles, abstracts and notes. To eliminate extraneous records, you will need to learn some of the more advanced searching techniques. It is also possible to narrow down a search by utilizing Boolean connecting terms, so if you were to enter the search **prozac and adolescents**, you would significantly reduce the number of records retrieved.

By selecting a number from the records list in Figure 7.6, you would see a complete record such as in Figure 7.7.

This record gives you all the usual index information as well as an abstract. Database records, as mentioned previously, are composed of fields; the most common fields used in indexes being author, title, and subject. Subject headings, however, are often called *descriptors* in electronic databases, as you can see in Figure 7.7. Every good index database provides some sort of subject field, although the name given to this field may differ. For example, a medical database, *Medline*, calls its subject headings MESHs (medical subject headings).

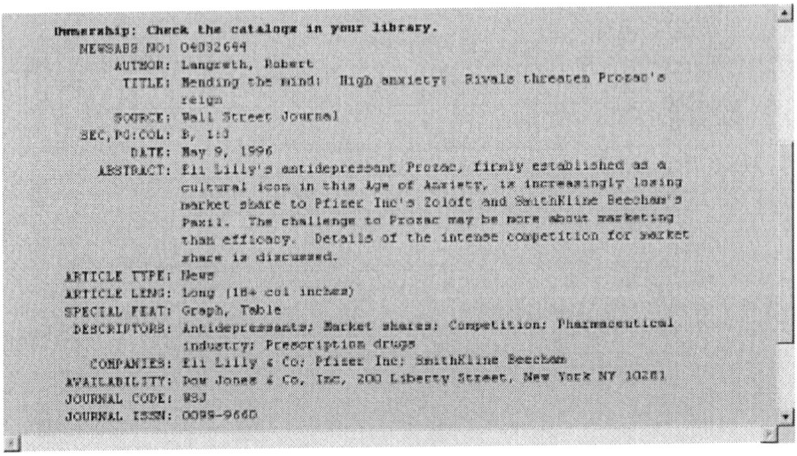
Ownership: Check the catalogs in your library.
NEWSABS NO: 04032644
AUTHOR: Langreth, Robert
TITLE: Mending the mind: High anxiety: Rivals threaten Prozac's reign
SOURCE: Wall Street Journal
SEC,PG:COL: B, 1:3
DATE: May 9, 1996
ABSTRACT: Eli Lilly's antidepressant Prozac, firmly established as a cultural icon in this Age of Anxiety, is increasingly losing market share to Pfizer Inc's Zoloft and SmithKline Beecham's Paxil. The challenge to Prozac may be more about marketing than efficacy. Details of the intense competition for market share is discussed.
ARTICLE TYPE: News
ARTICLE LENG: Long (18+ col inches)
SPECIAL FEAT: Graph, Table
DESCRIPTORS: Antidepressants; Market shares; Competition; Pharmaceutical industry; Prescription drugs
COMPANIES: Eli Lilly & Co; Pfizer Inc; SmithKline Beecham
AVAILABILITY: Dow Jones & Co, Inc, 200 Liberty Street, New York NY 10281
JOURNAL CODE: WSJ
JOURNAL ISSN: 0099-9660

Figure 7.7: A typical FirstSearch record.

A Basic Keyword Search Using *PsycLIT*

PsycLIT, the electronic version of *Psychological Abstracts*, carries citations for articles in psychology journals. This example uses the SilverPlatter CD-ROM version for Windows.

Suppose you wanted to locate articles in psychology journals pertaining to the effects of television violence upon children. A basic search for this topic would simply be **children and television and violence**, which you would enter in the "Search For" box as illustrated in Figure 7.8 below. It is important to note that in addition to looking for these words as subject headings (or descriptors, as they're called in this database), *PsycLIT* automatically searches the abstract of the article as well as every other part of the citation record, so this is really a keyword search. This search in *PsycLIT* results in a set of thirty-five records as shown in the highlighted set number 4 in Figure 7.8. The other sets tell you how many times each individual word was found. The brief citation list begins at the bottom of the screen. In Figure 7.9 you'll find a sample *PsycLIT* record found through this

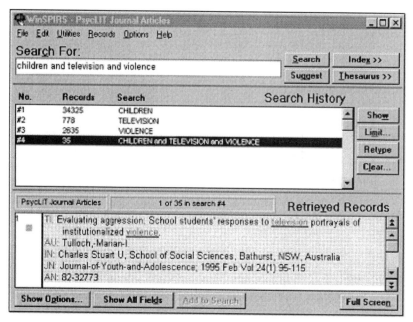

Figure 7.8: *PsycLIT* search screen displaying results of a search.
© 1986–1995 American Psychological Association
© 1986–1995 Silver Platter International N.V.

search displayed in full format. It's a bit more complex than the entries we have seen in previous examples, but it really isn't that hard to understand. Again, it's just a record composed of fields; these fields are designated by codes. TI is obviously the title of the article; AU is the author. Another important field is JN, the journal information, which tells you in which issue of a particular periodical you can find the article. Because many journal indexes are international in their coverage, LA indicates in what language the article is written. AB is the abstract or summary of the article. KP stands for "key phrase" and simply provides some important keywords not in the official descriptor field (DE). Most of the other lines are really not essential for the typical user; in fact, I still don't even know what they all mean.

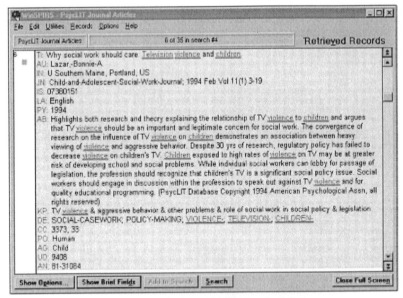

Figure 7.9: Sample *PsycLIT* citation in full format.

ADVANCED SEARCHING TECHNIQUES

A More Complicated Search Using *Readers' Guide Abstracts*

The previous search examples were relatively simple. But let's say that you want to find articles on a more complex topic. To return to a topic we had trouble with in chapter 5 using the print version of *Readers' Guide*, suppose you needed to know how advertising agencies are targeting African Americans with ads for both cigarettes and alcohol. Although *Readers' Guide* will provide some citations on this topic, remember that other indexes might also be helpful, like *Wilson Business Abstracts* or even *PsycLIT*. This topic previously presented a problem when using the print *Readers' Guide* because a single subject term cannot possibly define it; there are too many terms involved here: advertising, cigarettes, alcohol, and African Americans (or blacks). Since a single subject search will be inefficient, select "Multiple subject search" from the main menu to perform this complex search, and enter your search terms in the screen provided, as in Figure 7.10.

Filling in this screen allows you to do a very detailed search. The more information you enter, the narrower your search will become and the fewer records you will find that match all of your search criteria. The subject lines are the most essential and most frequently used, because entering terms on these lines defines your topic. You don't have to enter subject terms on all three lines, however, unless this is necessary. The other lines can be filled in if you want to limit the search to a certain periodical, or year, or to make your search more precise in a variety of ways. If you enter "Y" in the line which says "Type Y to search Abstracts," you will broaden your search, because the terms entered in the subject lines will be found within the abstracts in addition to being found in the subject headings and titles, which are automatically searched. Be careful when doing something like this, however, since it can result in the retrieval of ir-

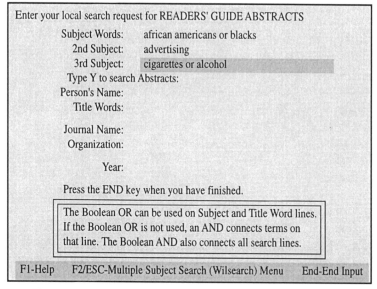

Figure 7.10: *Readers' Guide* "Multiple subject search" screen.

relevant material, as we saw in the FirstSearch example for articles about Prozac.

Multiple subject searching is essentially keyword searching. The first keyword for this example is **African Americans**, which is entered on the first subject line. But always consider whether there are common synonyms for each keyword. In this case, **blacks** is an obvious synonym. So the first part of this search could be **african americans or blacks** (note that it is usually not necessary to enter capital letters or hyphens when searching an electronic database). Remember that, by using *or*, either one of the terms indicated will be found. Next, the term **advertising** definitely needs to be included, so it is put on the second subject line. The connecting term *and* is implied in this database, meaning that *and* connects the search lines—in this case, your search so far is: **(african americans or blacks) and advertising**. In addition, terms on the same line are automatically connected with *and* if an *or* is not inserted between them. This search also must include **alcohol** or **cigarettes** since you're interested in both products, so again you employ the connecting term *or* and enter **alcohol or cigarettes** on the third subject line. The results of this search are displayed in Figure 7.11.

The box at the bottom of the screen tells you how many articles have been found that meet your search specifications. Above this, you see how many times each term was found. For example, **advertising** was found 2,675 times. This is really not important except to help identify ineffective terms when a search retrieves too few records or none at all. If one of the specified terms is found zero times, it may simply be misspelled. If not, think of a synonymous term, or simply eliminate it from the search altogether.

One word of caution: you may sometimes find that the records you retrieve are not at all what you're looking for. In the search above, the first article found happens to be titled, "Silver Screen, Black Lungs," which is about the subliminal promotion of cigarettes in motion pictures. The terms

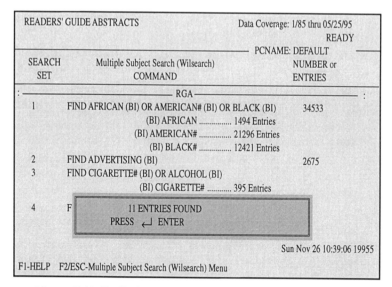

Figure 7.11: Preliminary results of a multiple subject search in *Readers' Guide*.

advertising and **cigarettes** do appear in the subject headings; **black**, however is found out of context in the title. Remember that the terms you specify in the subject lines of a *Readers' Guide* multiple subject search are located in the subject headings as well as the titles of articles, but nowhere else in the record unless you instruct the computer to search abstracts. *Readers' Guide* also searches plural and singular forms of a search term ending in **s** automatically, so this search retrieved records containing both **black** and **blacks**.

The Importance of Choosing Appropriate Terms: An Example from *PsycLIT*

In *PsycLIT* and many other databases, as I mentioned, subject headings are called descriptors. The descriptor field is especially important. Determining appropriate descriptor terms to search is the most essential part of conducting an effective search. Let's say you wanted to find some articles in psychology journals concerning drug abuse among teenagers. Easy enough, you think—just enter the main terms with a search statement like **teenagers and drug abuse**. The computer then searches all the fields, including the often lengthy abstracts, of all the records in the database and finds seventeen records that contain both of these terms. But is this really all there is in this whole database? It doesn't seem like very many.

Many computerized indexes contain a thesaurus, which is very similar to the books of synonyms you may often use to find colorful words to jazz up your writing. This type of electronic thesaurus, however, serves a more basic purpose, containing words that are used as descriptors to categorize records in a particular database, along with all the possible synonyms and related terms for these words. So, if you look up **teenagers** in the *PsycLIT* thesaurus, you get the screen in Figure 7.12.

This screen is simply telling you that in order to conduct a more effective search, you should be using the term **adolescents** instead of **teenagers**. **Adolescents** is an official descriptor, whereas **teenagers** is not. While still in the thesaurus with the term **adolescents** highlighted, you could select the highlighted heading to see a more detailed description of the term **adolescents** that will include broader, narrower, and related terms that you might want to try in order to refine your search. This listing is similar to the format of the *Library of Congress Subject Headings*. When you look up **drug abuse** in the thesaurus, it appears in the list without any *see* reference, which basically means that it is an official descriptor. If you now perform a search for **adolescents and drug abuse**, you get 476 entries—much more than the seventeen that were found when **teenagers** and **drug abuse** were the terms. This significant increase in the number of citations found demonstrates how important it is to choose the right search terms.

You can also determine descriptors indirectly without using the thesaurus. First, do a search like **teenagers and drug abuse**. Then browse through the descriptor fields of the seventeen records that were found. You will see that many

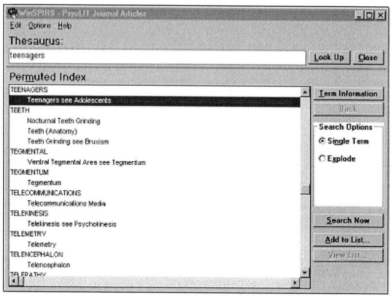

Figure 7.12: Entry for **teenagers** in the *PsycLIT* thesaurus.
© 1986–1995 American Psychological Association
© 1986–1995 Silver Platter International N.V.

of the records have **adolescents**, rather than **teenagers**, in the descriptor field.

Field-Specific Searching

The search for drug abuse among adolescents was so successful, yielding almost five hundred records, that you might consider it too successful. The resultant set of records will be a bit unwieldy to deal with. When your search results in such a large set, it is a good idea to eliminate some of the less relevant citations by specifying that your search terms only be found in descriptor fields. Otherwise, as I've already mentioned, the computer will search for them in all the fields of a record including the abstracts, which usually brings up some material that is a bit irrelevant.

If you look up **adolescents and drug abuse** in the descriptor field only (I'll explain how to do this next), 130 records are found. Many of the records eliminated from the original set of 476 probably mentioned the terms **drug abuse** and **adolescents** in the abstract, but the main focus of the article was not really on this topic. By limiting the search to the descriptor field, you access the most pertinent group of articles. This method of field-specific searching is very effective when you want to conduct a more precise search and decrease the number of records you must go through.

In this version of *PsycLIT*, you limit your search to the descriptor field by entering the words **in de** (for "in descriptor") after your search terms; other databases employ variations of this method. The most important thing is to understand the concept of field-specific searching rather than the specific ways in which you do this in each database, so don't try and memorize the following instructions; they're only intended to demonstrate a principle. There are various ways of entering **in de** in *PsycLIT*. First, you can add **in de** to your initial search statement like this: **adolescents in de and drug abuse in de**, or use **(adolescents and drug abuse) in de**, which is interpreted the same way by the computer and results in 130 records. Another method is to specify the **in de** command following your initial search, as illustrated in Figure 7.13. In other words, after locating the set of 476 articles for drug abuse among adolescents (set number 8), you could perform a new search by entering **#8 in de** to search easily for all the terms in the descriptor field without having to type them again. This creates set number 9 which also has 130 records. Doing it this way can be more practical because sometimes you don't know that you want to limit to the descriptor field until you've done a general search and found too much. The ability to manipulate previously created sets is a nice advanced feature of many databases.

Field-specific searching is not limited to the descriptor field. You could also look for terms only in the title of the article; or you can combine a descriptor search with a particular journal or author. But to get into the details of these advanced searching techniques, which you will probably not need to use very often, would make this a rather lengthy

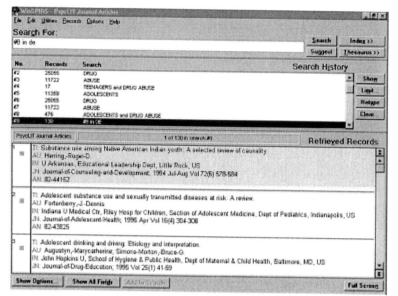

Figure 7.13: Combining sets to perform a
descriptor field search in *PsycLIT*.
© 1986–1995 American Psychological Association
© 1986–1995 Silver Platter International N.V.

chapter. A librarian should be able to show you how to do these things.

Although it may seem like I have gotten a bit far into the specifics of searching a particular database that you might not even use, as I said before, the underlying principles by which most electronic databases are searched remain basically the same. In general, the most effective searches are those that use the most appropriate terminology and are limited to certain fields of the record.

To return to the analogy I offered in the beginning of this chapter, finding exactly what you want in an electronic database is like taking a good picture. You must be selective and then focus. With a camera, you carefully choose the object you want to photograph; then you focus the camera by turning the lens. With an electronic index, you carefully choose your terminology; then you focus by limiting your search to specific fields of the record.

Eight

Cruising the Internet

Since I've been comparing the research process to going on a road trip throughout this book, it's now time to discuss the Internet, which is often called the "information superhighway." Although still under construction, the Internet has the potential to profoundly affect the way we do research—in fact, it may redefine the nature of the library. But for now, despite the message you may be getting from the media or what you may be hearing from "cyberpunks" (those individuals who eat, sleep, and breathe computers), it remains a novelty that can hardly replace all the other sources discussed in this book.

Thus, the focus of this chapter will *not* be on the popular communication functions of the Internet such as e-mail, bulletin boards, and newsgroups; or technical aspects such as file transfer protocol. These subjects don't really fall into the scope of this book. Instead, this chapter will introduce you to finding information on the Internet using the *World Wide Web*, which is the most likely route your library uses if it provides access to the Internet.

The Internet resources to be discussed in this chapter belong to a vast body of publicly available, free information, which is what most people associate with the Internet. But remember that we have already looked at some resources that can be considered part of the Internet: these are the commercial online databases discussed in chapter 6, which charge your library a fee and/or require a password. Think of the "Net" this way: although much of your driving will be along free public roads, you'll probably have to pay a few tolls when you're on a long trip, or encounter some private roads on which you can't travel without authorization. This chapter is about the free public thoroughfares. It will provide a very brief and general introduction, which will give you a sense of what you'll see on the information superhighway and some basic directions for getting from one place to another. However, you may need more precise directions to reach your destination. There are plenty of books devoted exclusively to the Internet that you can refer to for more in-depth instructions as well as a lot of very current how-to information on the Internet itself.

WHAT IS THE INTERNET?

Most academic institutions in the country today are connected to the Internet, a global network of computers that links users at colleges and universities, government agencies, libraries, corporations, and homes, allowing them to communicate with one another and share informational resources electronically. If Internet access is available at your school, the campus computer center should be able to set you up with your own personal account, allowing you to send and receive e-mail as well as explore informational resources. In addition to individual access, however, many academic libraries provide public access to the Internet. For this, the library connects to the college's host computer. A host is basically an on-ramp to the information superhighway. This is the main computer to which all the other computers at the institution connect to get on the Internet. Once you're cruising the Internet, you'll probably want to find some information. In order to do this you must access a server, which is a computer at another institution that provides information. Think of a server as an exit ramp on the information superhighway.

At this stage in its development, the main problem with the Internet is its lack of adequate organization and its proliferation of useless information. Picture a big library in which the books are not arranged by call number, just sort of grouped together loosely by subject; this can make it difficult to find the exact location of the material you need. There are also many volumes containing information that wouldn't interest anyone other than the writer. It can be an amusing place through which to wander, but if you're looking for a specific piece of information, it can be a bit frustrating. Many of the things that I have discovered on the Internet, I found accidentally while looking for something else.

Because you can wander through the Internet so aimlessly and because there is so much junk out there, I consider the Internet to be the "icing on the cake" in your research rather than the first or only place to go. As it becomes better organized and more user friendly, however, I believe it will take on a more integral function as a research tool.

WHAT'S AVAILABLE ON THE INTERNET?

"Has Bill Clinton delivered any radio addresses in which he discussed smoking?"

"What are the lyrics to the classic *Schoolhouse Rock* song 'I'm Just a Bill'?"

"How many acres of rain forest are being destroyed per second?"

"How much should you tip your guide on a Costa Rican rain forest expedition?"

"Approximately what percentage of Americans are vegetarians?"

"How do you roast a pig?"

What do these questions have in common? Nothing really,

except that I found the answers to them while wandering around the Internet one afternoon. Sure, you might be able to find some of the answers elsewhere, perhaps using some of the sources I've described in this book, but I've chosen these diverse topics to demonstrate the wide range of information available on the Internet. There's everything from the immensely practical to the merely trivial, or, as the saying goes, "from the sublime to the ridiculous."

There is an unbelievable amount of information available on the Internet. New sources are added on a daily basis. As I have familiarized myself with this system, I have found such items as episode guides for *Cheers, Northern Exposure,* and the *Simpsons*; how-to information on such unrelated topics as lock-picking and hair-dyeing; and movie reviews by the Teen Movie Critic. Of course, I have also found more "serious" research sources such as the Web Museum, which provides a virtual computerized art gallery, and Thomas, a governmental information resource that includes such items as U.S. Census reports and White House press releases.

Since the Internet began as the Department of Defense's ARPAnet project in 1969, the government has always had a strong presence on the information superhighway. Just about every federal department and agency has contributed extensive information to this global network. As the Net has grown, academic institutions have made substantial amounts of information available online through Campus Wide Information Systems, which provide an electronic community bulletin board for colleges all over the country and the world and include information of interest to students at a particular school such as class schedules, course descriptions, campus activities, and dining-hall menus. You can often access the library online catalog and other library resources, as well as find weather information, restaurant and movie reviews, and cultural event schedules for the area. These Campus Wide Information systems are increasingly taking the form of home pages on the World Wide Web, which I will be discussing shortly.

Even though many library catalogs are available over the Internet, you still have to go to the library and get the books off the shelves. The exception to this rule, however, are books that are stored in electronic format and can be retrieved over the Internet. The complete text of classic works such as *Moby Dick, Alice in Wonderland, Tarzan of the Apes,* and hundreds of others are in the files of the Internet's *Project Gutenberg,* which is collecting and making available a variety of titles in an electronic format.

But there's still the problem of all the junk on the Internet. Many companies have realized the value of the Internet for promoting themselves and their products, so a great deal of what you find out there in cyberspace is really just advertising. Although many nonprofit organizations provide useful educational resources on the Internet, some of them also use it to spread propaganda. There are even individual Internet users out there who, in increasing numbers, are posting resumes, wedding pictures, bad poetry, and other such personal items. Grammar school students can even put their book reports and information about their science projects on the Internet. It can be a lot to muddle through while trying to find what you really need.

THE WORLD WIDE WEB: A VEHICLE FOR CRUISING THE INTERNET

So how do you find what you need in this massive and messy collection of information? The most popular way of taking advantage of the wealth of Internet resources is by using the World Wide Web, a graphical interface that presents information in a hypertext format, allowing you to easily explore the resources available.

The Web's Predecessors

To fully understand and appreciate the Web, let me first offer a brief history of the Internet tools that preceded it. Before the Web emerged as the premier vehicle for cruising the Internet, information was commonly accessed using what are known as Gophers. A Gopher provides a hierarchically arranged series of menus from which you can select to narrow in on your topic and ultimately find a text file containing the information you need. The first Gopher was designed way back in 1991 (a very long time ago, as far as Internet development is concerned) by some computer scientists at the University of Minnesota where, appropriately, the gopher is the school mascot. Although Gophers are quickly being replaced by Web sites, you still encounter them occasionally.

Prior to Gopher, the only way of retrieving information was to connect directly to a particular institution's server by using a command called Telnet. This presupposed, however, that you knew which server would have the information you needed, and also that you knew its address as well as a username and password. Telnet was adequate when there were only a few computers hooked up to the Internet. Scientists or government officials would just inform the appropriate people about a particular server and give them the address, username, and password. But as more organizations became part of the Internet, Telnet alone became insufficient.

Gopher, unlike Telnet, emerged as an Internet tool that allowed you to find information without having to know different addresses. The University of Minnesota mascot became an appropriate symbol for this tool, since it enabled you to "go for" information by selecting from a menu. And, like the animal, it burrowed—not through dirt, but through the loose hierarchical levels of information on the Internet.

To provide my own metaphor, imagine you're driving along Route 66 in Kingman, Arizona. Your ultimate destination is Tucson. Even if you're unfamiliar with this area, just look at a map and you'll see that in order to get to Tucson, you have to get on 40 East, then take 93 South and then 60 East into Phoenix, where you can pick up 10 East, which goes through Tucson. In the same way, it may take a few steps to get to the resource that you want using Gopher.

But wouldn't it be nice to be able to get from Kingman to Tucson directly without all of those intervening highways? After all, the shortest distance between two points is a straight line. This is what the World Wide Web can do, figuratively speaking, because it provides those handy hypertext links (we'll get to them shortly). Another reason for the Web's sudden popularity is its capability of displaying both text and pictures in a much more user-friendly and attractive format.

Web Sites and Home Pages

The World Wide Web consists of *Web sites*, which are sources for information. Each Web site has a *home page*, or introductory screen from which to begin your exploring. A home page is like a table of contents. For instance, it is becoming commonplace for a college or university to have a home page from which you can connect to many different departments of the institution, including the library. Even some students have their own Web sites and home pages! If you've watched television recently or just browsed through a newspaper or magazine, you've probably also seen companies or organizations advertising their World Wide Web addresses, which you need to access their home page. These addresses are called *URLs*, or *uniform resource locators*, and generally begin with **www** followed by the particular address; they end with such three letter codes as **edu** for schools, **com** for companies, and **org** for other organizations. Although you may see an address begin with **http://** it is no longer necessary to enter this part of the URL in order to access the Web site.

The sections of the address are separated by "dots." As an example of a typical home page, let's take a look at the Rainforest Action Network's (RAN) Web site by entering **www.ran.org** in the location box.

From this home page (see Figure 8.1) you simply click on any of the options displayed ("About RAN," "Rainforest

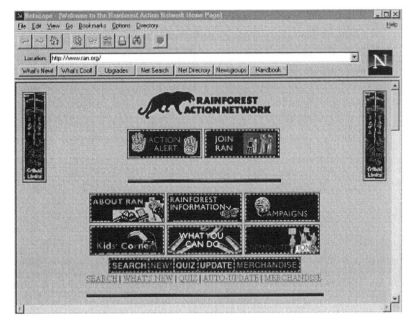

Figure 8.1: The Rainforest Action Network's home page.

Information," "Campaigns," and so on) and quickly proceed to a specific area of information. These options are commonly referred to as *links*, because they link you to another page within the Web site or to another Web site entirely. You can also scroll up and down the page to browse. If you wanted to go to another home page, you could just enter another URL in the location box at the top of the screen.

Hypertext

Let's say you're looking in a book for information on your topic. You could read the book from cover to cover in a linear fashion, or you could check the index in the back of the book to determine which pages contain the specific information you need. While looking in the index, you might see related topics listed with their appropriate page numbers. Referring to these different pages and flipping back and forth in a book using the index is the hypertextual way to read. This is the sort of thing that the World Wide Web allows you to do in a computerized context.

To see how this works, let's look at the screen in Figure 8.2, which can be accessed through NASA's home page. Notice in the second line under Mission Objective that the word **moon** is highlighted. When you click on this highlighted term, you can immediately access a Web site with information about the moon (see Figure 8.3).

This Web site has nothing to do with NASA; it's located on a server at a college in Arizona. In this screen notice that in the line following the second bullet, the name **Artemis** is highlighted. If you click on this name, you'll be brought to a Web site at another location that discusses Greek mythology. This is the nature of hypertext. It gives you the ability to jump around and follow various topics that may have only loose connections.

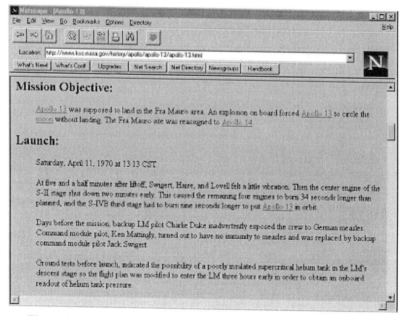

Figure 8.2: Page from the NASA Web site providing information on Apollo 13 and hypertext links to related topics.

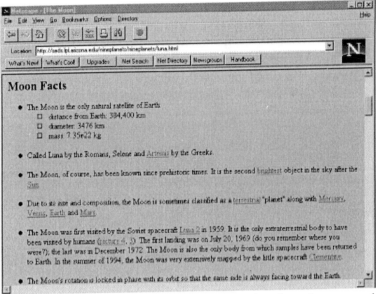

Figure 8.3: A Web page providing basic information about the moon and hypertext links to related topics.

Browsers

World Wide Web pages do not always have the same appearance as the screens I have reprinted so far in this chapter. While the content of the World Wide Web (the information itself) is stored on an institution's server, the format this information takes on your screen is created by the software loaded on the computer you're using. All of the Web screens that have been displayed so far derive their format from Netscape Navigator software, which is a browsing tool or *browser* that is the most popular way of looking at the World Wide Web. Other graphical browsers that you might encounter are NCSA Mosaic and Microsoft's Internet Explorer.

The computers at some colleges, however, cannot yet support graphical browsers, so you may encounter a Web browser called *Lynx*, which provides only the text portions of the information available through the Web. Although Lynx cannot display graphics it still has hypertext capabilities.

To show you the difference, first look at the White House home page as seen through Lynx (Figure 8.4) then at the same page as seen with Netscape (Figure 8.5). Quite a difference, don't you think? Lynx does have the benefit of being a bit faster, because it can take a great deal of time to access some of the fancy graphics seen through Netscape.

Searching the World Wide Web

Just as browsing through a library for the information you want is not the most effective way to conduct research, so jumping from link to link on the Web often sends you flying off on amusing yet time-consuming tangents. A more efficient way of accessing information is to enter the URL for a specific Web site's home page. But it's hard to know exactly what information you'll find at a given Web site unless you've been there before; it's also difficult to determine the URL itself unless you've heard about it from an outside source. Fortunately, there are more effective ways of finding information on the World Wide Web.

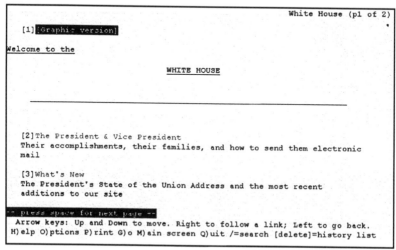

Figure 8.4: White House home page accessed with Lynx.

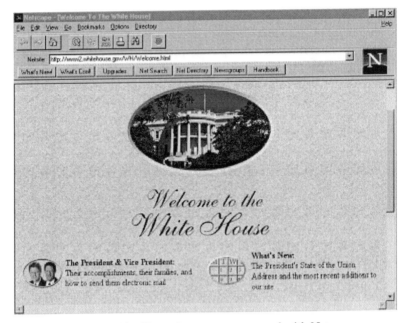

Figure 8.5: White House home page accessed with Netscape.

One way is by using a directory. This is similar to a Gopher, because it arranges Web sites hierarchically. Rather than acting like an index, a directory is more like the table of contents for a book, or even like a home page for the Web itself. One of the most popular Web directories, Yahoo!, categorizes thousands of home pages under a small number of main subject groups. To use Yahoo! go to its own home page (see Figure 8.6) by entering the URL **www.yahoo.com** (or simply **yahoo**; when entering a company's URL, it is no longer necessary to enter the **www** or the **.com**)

You will notice that Yahoo! does have a keyword search option right in the middle of the screen, but this is not as effective as some of the keyword indexes I will be discussing next because Yahoo! doesn't cover that much of the Web to begin with. It only indexes selected sites and is best when you have a general topic or just want to browse. If you wanted information on photography, for example, you could

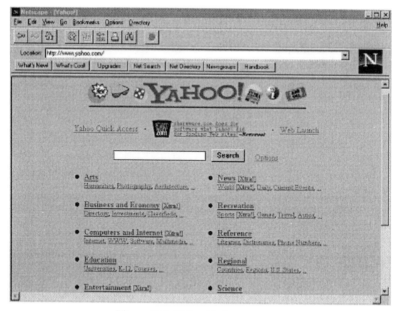

Figure 8.6: Yahoo!'s home page.

click on the heading "Arts," which would bring you to a submenu of many arts-related topics.

When your informational need is more specific, there are more effective ways of finding what you need on the Web. Quite a few companies have recently emerged that have developed what are called *search engines* to catalog Web resources. Some of the more popular search engines are Lycos, Alta Vista, InfoSeek, Excite, and WebCrawler. Each has its own home page and URL (see Table 8.1) and, despite some overlap, covers a different set of Web sites and serves a different purpose. For instance, Alta Vista covers the highest proportion of the Web, while Excite only indexes the most popular Web sites. Therefore, Alta Vista is appropriate for more obscure topics, while Excite will probably be sufficient for more common topics. There is currently no single search engine that indexes the entire World Wide Web. Although Lycos claims to index over 90 percent of the Web and is generally the one I use first, I would suggest trying out some

Table 8.1: Overview of Web Search Engines

Name	Address	When To Use It
Alta Vista	http://altavista.digital.com	Best when you're looking up less common topics since it searches complete text of most sites.
Excite	http://www.excite.com	Since it only searches complete text of the most popular sites, it's good for looking up mainstream topics that are widely discussed and for getting in-depth reviews of these sites.
InfoSeek	http://guide.infoseek.com	When you want to search precisely a limited portion of the Web.
Lycos	http://www.lycos.com	When you want to search as much of the Web as possible without having to search the complete text of sites.
Magellan	http://www.mckinley.com	When you want to search a small portion of the Web and be provided with reviews of the sites found.
Open Text	http://www.opentext.com	When you want to search a particular portion of the Web with complex searches that retrieve highly relevant material.
WebCrawler	http://webcrawler.com	Like Excite, use it for common popular topics.
Yahoo!	http://www.yahoo.com	When your topic is somewhat broad and you just want to browse through hierarchically arranged categories of sites

of the other search engines if Lycos doesn't get you what you need. Choosing the appropriate search engine is like selecting a periodical index; you must consider your topic and the purpose of each search engine, and then use the ones that will satisfy your informational needs. Table 8.1 can help you get started.

All Web search engines search the titles of home pages and their URLs for the words you specify. Most also search section headings within a home page. Each search engine (Lycos, WebCrawler, InfoSeek, etc.) works a little differently but most operate along the principles of Boolean searching. Some, like Alta Vista, even search the complete text, but this might not be such a good thing because it can retrieve a great deal of junk unless you are proficient with advanced searching techniques. The records you retrieve usually include a description or abstract. By clicking on the title of a particular record, you will be sent to the Web site being described.

Using Lycos

Let's say you needed some information regarding rain forests, specifically the rate at which they are being destroyed. How would you find information on this topic using the World Wide Web? Well, you could start in Yahoo!, but I tried this and found myself wandering around a bit aimlessly even after I selected the main category "Society and Culture" and the submenu option "Environment and Nature." You could also enter the URL for an organization concerned with rain forests if you just happened to know an address. But your final and perhaps best option would be to use a search engine.

Let's try Lycos. First, connect with the home page for Lycos by entering the URL **www.lycos.com**. This brings up the basic Lycos search form (although it changes quite frequently, most of the alterations so far have been superficial) shown in Figure 8.7. Just enter words that define your topic in the box in the middle of the screen after "Find:" and then click on "Go Get It." Notice that under this box there are three options: "lycos catalog," "a2z directory," and "point reviews." The Lycos catalog should be your initial selection because it performs the most comprehensive search of the Web. The a2z directory is similar to Yahoo!'s hierarchical directory approach to organizing Web sites and is more selective; point reviews are even more selective, highlighting only what the designers consider to be the best sites and providing in-depth reviews of these sites.

You will find that many of the rules that have already been discussed in this book concerning searching electronic databases also apply to the Internet. When you enter a string of words in the Lycos search box, the term *or* is automatically inserted between them. There is a more advanced search screen that will be displayed if you click on "Enhance your search" (this command appears on the left side of the screen in Figure 8.7).

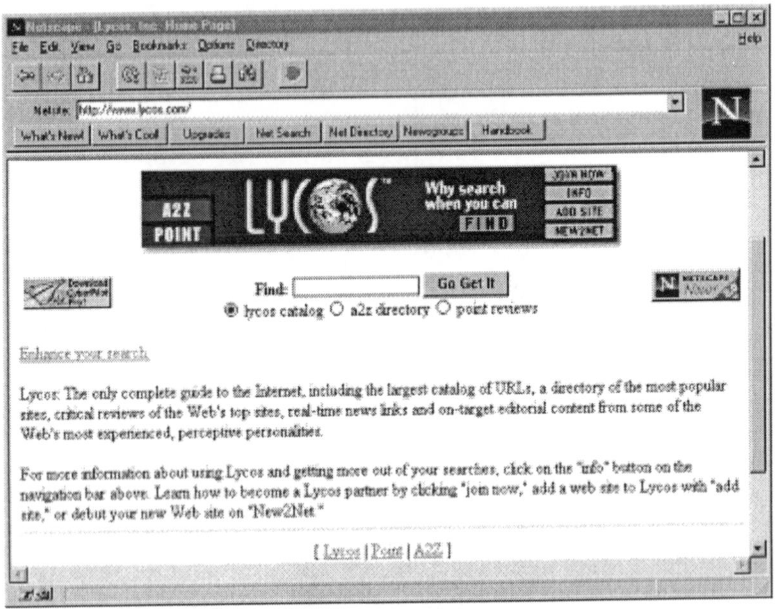

Figure 8.7: Lycos home page.

On this enhanced search screen (see Figure 8.8) you can specify your "Search Options" and "Display Options." For example, when searching for rain forest destruction, you can specify that you want all the terms located, thus changing the automatic *or* to an *and*. You do this by clicking the arrow after "match any term (OR)," which brings up a menu allowing you to select "match all terms (AND)" or even to indicate that you want to find at least two of the three terms. In the same way, you can also specify how many entries you want to display at a time; if you don't specify, you'll see ten. There are a variety of other options but, for most of your needs, the simple search screen will be sufficient, so let's return to that.

Let's say you entered **rain forests** in the "Find" box and clicked the "Go Get It" button. This retrieves 44,789 records, but remember that many of these records will have only the

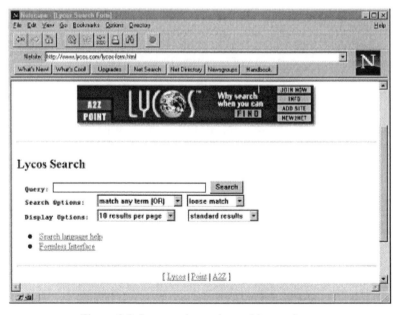

Figure 8.8: Lycos enhanced searching options.

word **rain** or the word **forest** because *or* is automatically inserted between the terms. In some other search engines, you can put a phrase in quotations in order for it to be found as a phrase rather than separate words, but this doesn't work in Lycos yet. And, since Lycos automatically truncates, some of the records will even have the word **rainbow**. You obviously don't want to look through thousands of records, many of which will be irrelevant. Fortunately, Lycos and some of the other search engines rank the items found by their relevance. This means that the records containing both words in the exact form they were specified always appear first. It also means that records in which these two terms appear side by side have precedence, and records in which the terms appear more than once will be closer to the top of the list.

Actually, you could have entered this search in a variety of ways. The singular **rain forest** retrieves over ten thousand more records than the plural **rain forests** because **forestry** becomes a search term due to the automatic truncation. The fifth entry retrieved for this search describes a fifth grader's science report. Although this search does retrieve some information on rain forests, it doesn't exactly address the research question concerning destruction. The other problem is that many times **rain forest** (two words) is spelled **rainforest** (one word). According to my Webster's dictionary, the latter is incorrect, but the Web is a "brave new world" where there are no official subject headings used to index it.

You could insert another term in the box, perhaps searching for **rain forest destruction** as well as for **rainforest destruction**. The second entry retrieved by **rainforest destruction** points you to a Web site that has come up before—the Rainforest Action Network (see Figure 8.9). If you click on the heading, you will actually be transported to the pertinent part of RAN's Web site (Figure 8.10).

By the way, **rain forest destruction** (three words) also retrieves this record, but some of the other entries in the top ten list are irrelevant (such as one about acid rain), so in this

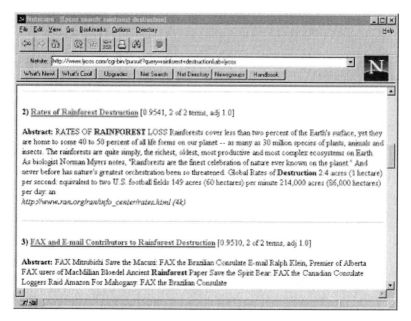

Figure 8.9: Web site found through Lycos under **rainforest destruction**.

case it's actually more effective to search for a misspelled term!

It would take an entire book to explain how each search engine works, because each works a bit differently. And because another characteristic of the Internet is how rapidly things change, the best way to find out how to use a specific search engine is to get online help. After entering one of the URLs displayed in Table 8.1 and connecting to a search engine, click on the "help" option. This will tell you whether *or* is implied between terms (as in Lycos) or *and* (as in WebCrawler), how the entries are ranked, and whether or not truncation is automatic.

Figure 8.10: RAN Web site containing information on
rain forest destruction.

ROADBLOCKS ON THE INTERNET

Major highways are designed to allow drivers to get from
one place to another as quickly as possible. But even on a
highway, you often meet obstacles that can slow you down.
As you find yourself stuck in the middle of a traffic jam due
to road construction, an accident, or just too many cars, you
may wish you had taken a back road instead.

The Internet has its own kinds of roadblocks. You may get
frustrated while using it as you encounter menu options that
lead to an unavailable resource, or slow response time due
to too many people using it, or just a lot of garbage in the
middle of the road. After selecting what sounds like a great
resource, you may be disappointed to receive messages like
"unable to connect to host," "permission denied," or "file not
found." Something may be there one day and gone the next.
The Internet is still very much under construction and has

a long way to go before it reaches its maximum potential. So you need to have some patience with it. Realize that it's not the glamourous one-stop shopping mall for every information need. Sometimes it's much easier to just pull a book off the shelf and open it up.

As I told you in the beginning of this chapter, my intention has been to show you what you might see along the road rather than how to drive the car. If you are interested in exploring the Internet further, you should go to your campus computer center to discover what access options you have as well as to get more detailed instruction on how to actually use these tools and others that are beyond the scope of this book. Your library may also provide access and instruction. You now have enough background to approach some of the recently published Internet books that often assume you already know a bit about the subject. But the best way to learn about the Internet is to get out there and go cruising. In time, it will become familiar territory.

Nine

The Trip Home

I nevitably after a long road trip, I like to think back upon where I've been and what I've seen. I might make some evaluations about what I liked and didn't like and if I'd want to travel the same route again in the future. Being a writer, I often feel compelled to write to preserve a record of the trip.

We've traveled a long road together since the beginning of this book. And along the way I've given you many directions, pointed out many sights, and tried to impart to you a sense of familiarity with the world of research. With this background, I hope you feel prepared to take the wheel confidently and travel through the library.

LOOKING BACK DOWN THE ROAD

Whenever I'm lost on the road, however, I don't wander around too long before I stop for directions. I figure I can save a lot of time and frustration if I simply ask someone for help. In the same way, you should not hesitate to ask for help in your library. Even after reading this book you may find that there are times when you feel a bit lost. That's understandable, and that's why every library has a Reference Desk where you can go to find your way amid all the resources in the library.

When I'm on the road and stop for directions, I usually need to have them repeated in order for them to sink in sufficiently. So just to make sure that you're headed in the right way as you finish this book, let's review the basic directions I've given you for doing effective research.

First, you need to know where you're going and what you're looking for. In other words, ask yourself, "What's my topic?" Remember, it doesn't have to be written in stone. It may evolve as you find material that sparks your interest in a new direction. But it should become very clearly defined at some point. If possible, pick a topic that interests you, just as you would choose a vacation destination for its appeal.

With this decision made, you need to plan your route and learn to use the necessary electronic resources. Our basic plan started with searching the online catalog for books. This, of course, requires that you know how to use the online catalog in your library. Remember that keyword searching is a useful option if you have problems with subject searching. Once you have located some books in the library stacks and determined which ones will be most useful, see if any of these have bibliographies at the end. Such bibliographies can provide a list of other helpful sources.

If you can afford the time, Interlibrary Loan is a service that enables you to get books as well as articles from distant places. You may also be able to access catalogs for area libraries right from your own library. So if you can't find enough books in your library, maybe another library can help.

Consult some basic reference books, if necessary. These can provide you with an overview of your topic or a specific fact you might need to make a point. Some of the reference books I mentioned in chapter 4 may also be available in computerized format at your library.

After books, look for periodical articles on your topic. In fact, sometimes periodicals will provide the only source of information on a current or very narrow topic. Recall that you can consult CD-ROM or online indexes as well as print indexes. Determine what indexes are available and in what format at your library and select the most appropriate ones for your topic: CD-ROMs? online services? At which terminals do you access each? Or can you access them from your home computer? Table 5.1 may help you in picking the appropriate indexes, but remember the librarians are also important resources.

The Internet, as I mentioned, is the "icing on the cake." Depending on your topic, it may—or may not—be of use. There's a lot of junk on the World Wide Web, but you may be able to find some interesting information. The most effective way of searching for what you need on the Web is to use a search engine like Lycos, Alta Vista, or another one listed in Table 8.1.

EVALUATING WHAT YOU'VE FOUND

Doing research is not just about finding information; it's also about evaluating what you've found and figuring out if it will be useful. This is especially necessary in our present age of information glut. With the constantly increasing amount of information available and the powerful electronic tools we now have for accessing it, you may well discover, to your surprise and dismay, that you've overwhelmed yourself with too many resources.

Although I've placed this section on evaluation here at the end of this book, evaluating your sources should actually be an ongoing process rather than something you do after you've found everything you can on your topic. So as you locate material, keep asking yourself the following questions.

Who Wrote It?

An author with credentials or some sort of track record adds credibility to your resources. While you can't always find out much about the author, books usually contain brief biographies. With periodicals, remember that you don't want to rely exclusively on popular magazines. Articles from scholarly journals carry more weight and are generally written by experts in their field. Plus, these articles have been selected by the author's peers as worthy of publication.

An interesting phenomenon brought about by the Internet is that anyone can now be an author in this electronic forum. The movie reviews of the Teen Movie Critic are as accessible as those of Siskel and Ebert. Roger Davidson, a home-schooler teenager from Minneapolis, started his Teen Movie Critic Web site in order to share his thoughts on various films with other teens. His reviews have now become popular with adults. Book reports written by fifth graders and scholarly papers written by doctoral candidates can be found through the same Lycos search. But what is the value of information that has not had to go through the rigorous channels that published works must go through? You have to be careful not to take everything you find on the Internet as truth; more often it is just advertising, propaganda, or simply the opinion of the contributor.

Does It Really Address My Topic?

Perhaps the most fundamental question you should ask is whether each source really provides you with the information you need. Does it answer the main questions that you have about your topic? The records you find using indexes and online book catalogs do not always have enough information to evaluate the material cited. Even when you are given an abstract in an article citation or a table of contents in an online book record, you may not get a clear idea of what the source will really provide. The only way to do this will be to find the actual book or article and skim through it, noticing how much your topic is addressed. You might also want to look up your topic in the book's index to get a sense of how many pages are devoted to it. Even though the source may have sounded great initially, you may realize that it really won't help you. Don't select a source for the sake of having one more item to add to your bibliography or just because it is easier to get. The quality of your information is more important than the quantity.

Quality material may also not always be the easiest information to obtain if you might have to go to microfilm or use a print index. Although I am a staunch supporter of the new technology available in libraries today and the potential of the information superhighway, I also appreciate the value of informational byways. Even though the highways can be very useful when your primary goal is to get somewhere fast, it is often more interesting to explore the secondary roads when you have the time. Often, you discover things there that you might never have seen from the main road. Often, the only road to travel to get to your destination is the back road.

When Was It Written?

Sometimes it is important to have the most recent information available, especially for scientific and business-related topics. In such cases, as you search for material on your subject, you should keep in mind the date each item was written. This will help you to narrow your search and focus on the most valuable information. At other times, it is not necessary to have the most up-to-date material, particularly with historical, social science, and humanities topics. In fact, when researching such areas, the latest information may not be the greatest.

Most students, however, prefer more recent information, particularly periodical articles, because it is usually easier to obtain. As I pointed out, most of the older stuff is on microfilm, and to find citations for this material you may have to use a print index rather than an electronic one. With the emerging availability of recent full-text articles online, more people are opting for current information. While I have nothing against the convenience of full-text electronic sources,

I have observed that too many students rely exclusively on the limited sources available in this format. Remember that, just like cruising historic Route 66 is much more interesting than speeding along Interstate-40, sometimes the most interesting sites are off the beaten track. So don't always look for the fastest way to get the most recent information. You may miss out on some really good sources.

THE RECORD OF YOUR TRIP

Of course, the end product of all your research and the record of your trip is reflected in the paper or project that you complete for one of your classes. This book is not intended to teach you how to write a research paper, but it is an important part of your paper: the documentation—the footnotes and bibliography that give credit to the sources you used to write the paper. And since a frequent reference question is how to cite sources, I'd like to briefly discuss this.

There is no single method of citing sources. Your professor may request that you follow a certain format. Some common formats include the MLA (Modern Language Association) style and the APA (American Psychological Association) style. You should be able to find the following handbooks to show you how to use these styles in your library: *The MLA Handbook for Writers of Research Papers* and the *Publication Manual of the American Psychological Association*. If your professor does not specify a format, another good handbook is *The Chicago Manual of Style*. Any one of these will show you in great detail how to cite just about anything you could possibly want to cite (with the possible exception of Internet sources). The important thing is that, once you select a style, you should use it consistently in all of your citations.

A bibliography is a general list of the sources that you used to write your paper. Footnotes, to differentiate, are incorporated into the body of your paper. Immediately after you use a direct quote or paraphrase the thought of someone else, you must give credit to the source—including the exact page reference—with a footnote at the bottom of the page. Endnotes are a variation on footnotes that are collected at the end of the paper. But unlike a bibliography, they are more specific, citing the exact page numbers.

I'll just give you a few examples here that demonstrate some general rules of the road; refer to some of the handbooks listed above for more detailed information.

Citing Books

The basic components of a book citation are the author, the title, the publisher, and the place and date of publication. For example, here is a typical citation for a book:

Nelson, Rob. *Revolution X: A Survival Guide for Our Generation.* New York: Penguin Books, 1994.

But let's say you specifically quoted something written on page 95 of this book. Then you'd have to do a footnote or endnote, which has a slightly different format:

1. Rob Nelson, *Revolution X: A Survival Guide for Our Generation* (New York: Penguin Books, 1994), 95.

Notice the subtle differences in punctuation and indentation. It's enough to drive you crazy, but it must be done. There are many variations for citing books: your book may have two, three, or more authors; or no author but instead, an editor, as is the case with many reference works; it could be a multivolume work or a specific edition. In each of these cases, the citation is a little different. This is why there are so many handbooks dedicated to giving you examples of how to do citations.

If you cite the same source more than once in your paper, it gets a little easier. Let's say the footnote immediately following the one above cites something Nelson said on page 143. There is no need to repeat the entire citation. If you are folowing the *Chicago Manual of Style* you would just use "**ibid., 143.**" *Ibid.* stands for "ibidem," which in Latin means "in the same place." If there were an intervening footnote, however, you would have to use a shortened citation omitting the subtitle and all but the most essential information: "**Nelson,** *Revolution X,* **143.**"

Citing Periodicals

By now, you should be familiar with the basic components of a periodical article citation since they are included in all indexes: the author, the title of the article, the title of the periodical in which the article is published, the date of the issue and page numbers, and, in the case of a journal, the volume and issue numbers.

The format for your bibliography, however, is a bit different from what you've seen in indexes. Here's a sample bibliography citation for a magazine article:

Fischoff, Stuart. "Confessions of a TV Talk Show Shrink." *Psychology Today*, Sept./Oct. 1995, 38–45.

If you are citing a journal article, you must also include the volume and issue number, so the format would be like this:

Wexler, Mark N., and Ron Sept. "The Psycho-Social Significance of Trivia." *Journal of Popular Culture* 28 (2):1–11 (1994).

The citation above indicates that the article is in issue 2 of volume 28, pages 1 through 11. As with books, there are many variations in citing periodicals, so consult a style manual.

All of this citing is meant not only to give credit to the authors of the sources you used, but also, in theory, to enable a reader of your paper to locate these sources. Therefore it is very important to include accurate date and page information.

Citing Internet Sources

A growing dilemma is how to cite electronic sources such as something you find on the Internet or on a full-text CD-ROM. As new editions of style manuals are published, a standard way of citing such sources will, out of necessity, emerge. For citing World Wide Web sites, I have actually found the best guidelines on the Web itself. Janice R. Walker, an English professor at the University of South Florida, has suggested a format based on MLA principles that has been endorsed by the Alliance for Computers and Writing. She recommends that the citation include the author's name (when available), the title of the WWW page, the title of the whole site (if it differs from the page), the address, and the date visited. If you are confused about the difference between a Web page and a Web site, think of it this way: a page is like an article in a magazine; a site is the whole magazine. Following Walker's principles, here's how I would cite the Teen Movie Critic's review of *The Truth About Cats and Dogs*:

Davidson, Roger. "The Truth About Cats and Dogs." *Teen Movie Critic.* http://www.skypoint.com/members/magic/roger/06–10–96.html#truth   (1 July 1996).

And if you want to see Walker's complete style guide, refer to the following:

Walker, Janice R. "MLA-Style Citations of Electronic Sources." University of South Florida. http://www.cas.usf.

edu/english/walker/mla.html (1 July 1996).

RIDING OFF INTO THE SUNSET

During my Route 66 road trip, my friend and I drove nine hundred miles in two days. The road itself was really our destination, although we particularly wanted to see the old ghost town of Oatman, Arizona. In the course of our trek, referring to our tattered state map, it seemed that we had covered a lot of territory. When I looked at an atlas long after our trip, however, and looked at the maps of the country and the world, I realized that we had only explored a very small corner of the globe. Even were I to spend my lifetime on the road, I still would not be able to see it all.

It's the same way with information. Consider, for example, that approximately 50,000 books are published each year in the United States. That's 140 books a day! I'm lucky if I can read a book every couple of weeks. Over 10,000 magazines and journals are currently in print. Walking into an average sized library and looking at all of the books, magazines, and newspapers on the shelves can be intimidating. But just as you will never be able to explore every nook and cranny on Earth, you will never be able to absorb all the knowledge accumulated by the human race.

The important thing is to be able to pinpoint the specific information that addresses your needs. Having read this book, I hope you will now be able to do this more efficiently, saving yourself lots of time and frustration so that you can more fully enjoy your time at college. Like I said in the beginning of this book, my fondest college memories are those involving me and my friends in a car—not in a library. If you get your research done more efficiently, as you should using the techniques I have described in this book, maybe you can reward yourself for a job well done by taking a real road trip. Bon voyage!

Index

About the Author

Arlene Rodda Quaratiello wrote this book while working at the Emerson College Library in Boston as the Coordinator of Library Instruction. She received her MLS from Simmons College in 1993 and earned a BA in English from the College of the Holy Cross in 1988. She is a member of the American Library Association and the College Libraries and Instruction Sections of the Association of College and Research Libraries.

The College Student's Research Companion is Arlene's first book. She has also published articles in professional journals including *RQ* and *Computers in Libraries*. Originally from New Jersey, she now lives in Medford, MA with her husband Mark.

Metropolitan State University
Library Services
St. Paul, MN 55106